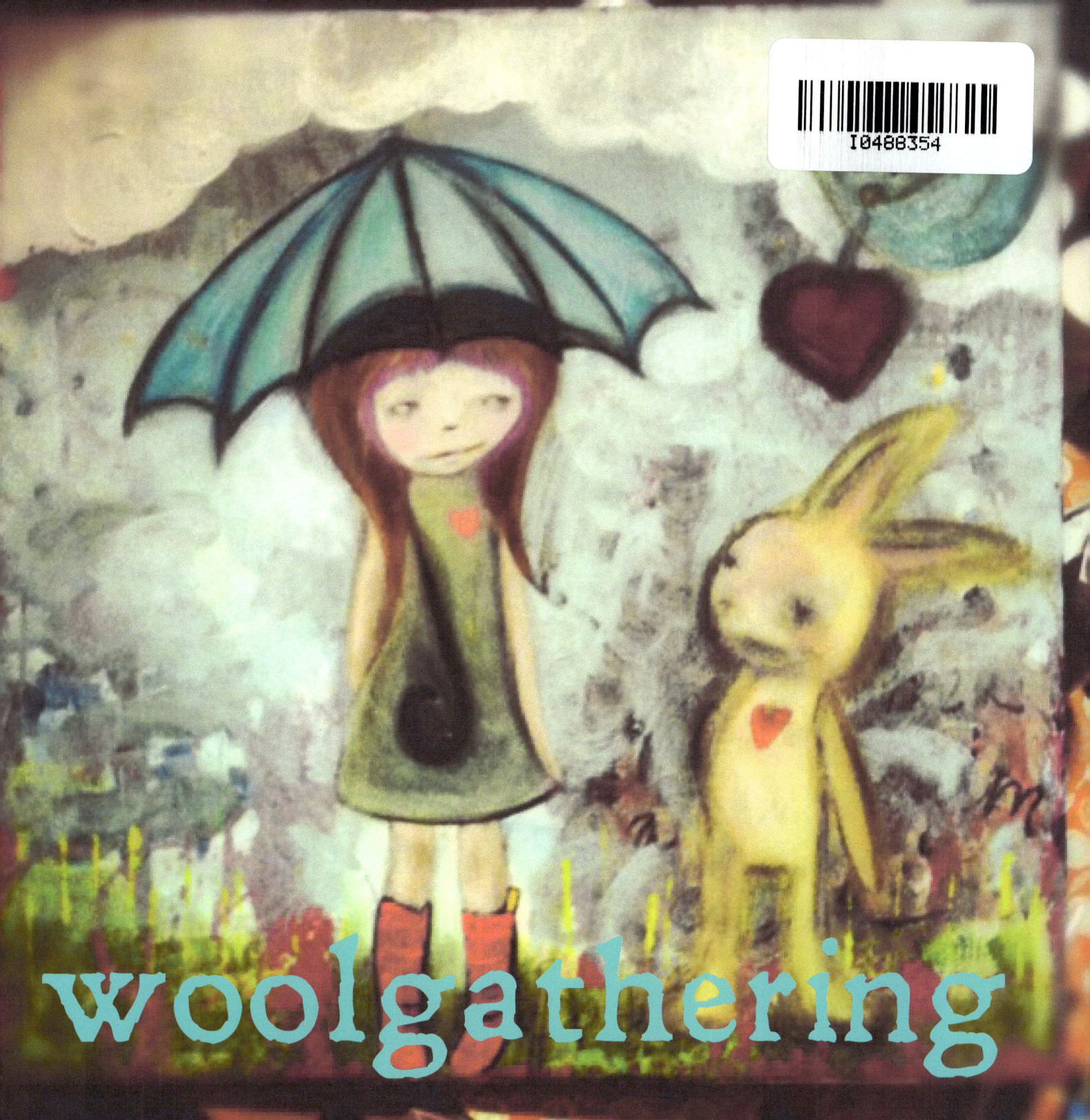

woolgathering

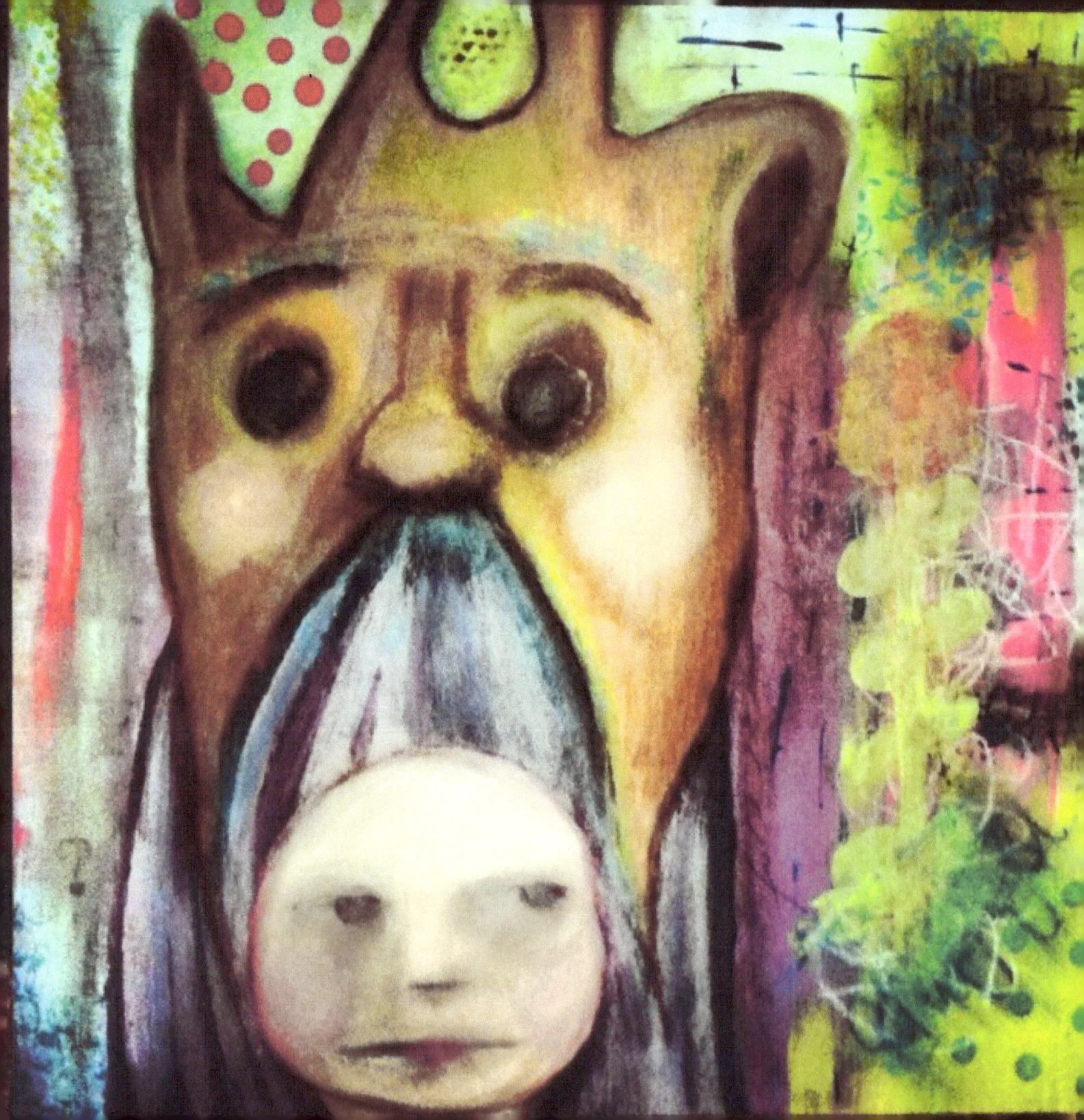

woolgathering:

bedtime stories for wayward grown-ups

written by corbyn hanson hightower
illustrated by valeri blossom

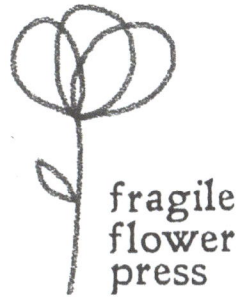

fragile flower press

Table of Contents

Parade fun: as the unicycle riders passed by,

your resident extrovert hollered,

"unicycles are mildly diverting!"

And without missing a beat,

one rider cheerfully shouted back at me,

"unicycles are entirely adequate!"

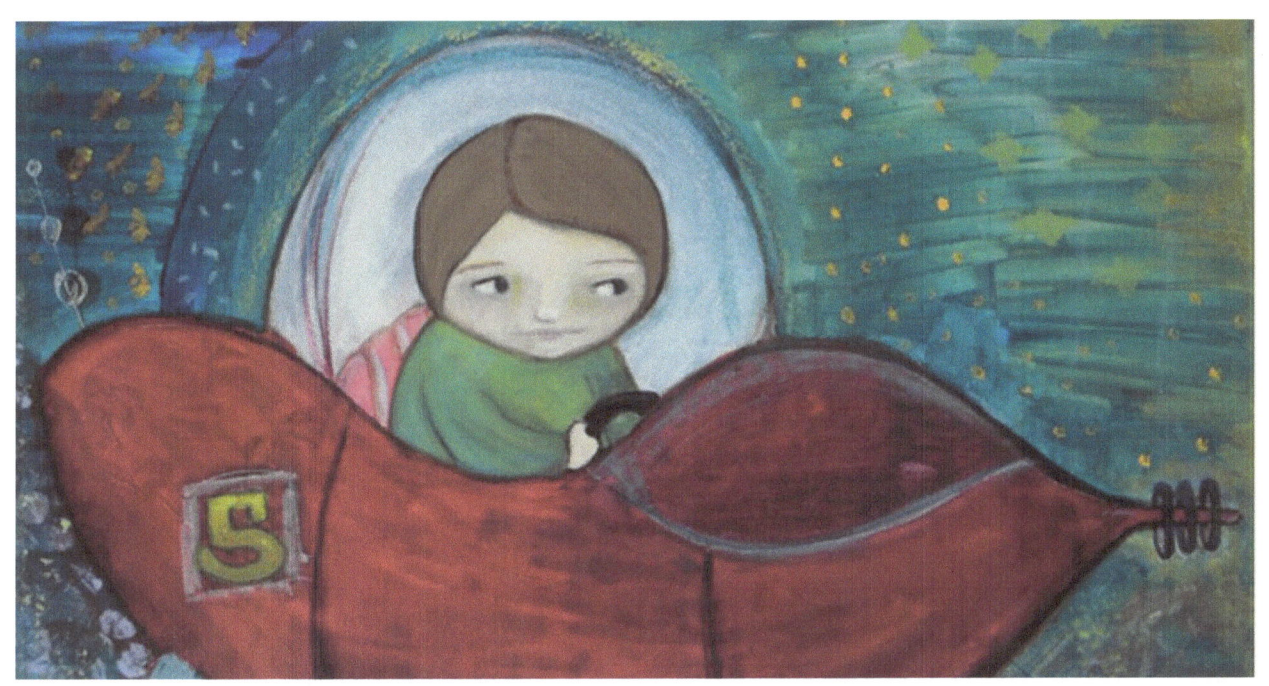

Meditations On No Longer Having a Car For My Family

Part I

The other day, I spotted a car in the parking lot that was exactly the same as the one we sold. It's not an uncommon make and model; I see them on the street all the time. But this time I was alone and walking past one, close enough to see the flecks of silver glittering in the paint job, and remembered with sudden vividness the feeling of having that heavy key in my hand the first time. I had felt like I was finally driving my life and that the future would happen at a certain speed and with a strong, straight trajectory. I started the motor and it sounded reassuringly steady. There weren't the now-familiar deviations down narrow dirt trails with unexpected sadnesses or big muddy places that I'd have to struggle to get through. This, my first new car, was a big, handsome, authoritative one, and it symbolized responsibility and security.

Youth had meant drunken bike rides back to my dorm room, early adulthood carried with it years of subway commuting from one mediocre job to another worse one and then coming home to my apartment in a seedy part of the city. In the years of early parenthood, when I was just beginning to build a career, I had driven dented minivans with missing hubcaps and six-digit odometers. I didn't miss our shining Honda as much as I thought I would, but I sometimes missed what it said about my life: that the road was solid beneath my wheels, that there were air bags at every side and in front of me, and that I was moving forward, driving my family down a clear and certain path.

It's hard to ignore the shifts of seasons and the presence of nature in our world when you are down and in it, simply accomplishing the most quotidian of tasks. You feel a subtle cold front blowing in on your way to the hardware store, you see the blackberries turning color while you patiently watch day after day, you see the mama cat's belly swell and then become a chorus of mewing heard in the brush, you navigate based on the location of the sun in the sky, and you notice it when the lavender-gray of evening comes just a little bit earlier than it did the day before. We live so close to the trailhead that we see the families that park nearby on the weekends for some scheduled and prearranged fun. They drive from some other part of town, they stop and buy bottles of water at the market, they circle for the closest place where they can stop and unhook their bicycles from the racks on the back of their cars, and then they visit nature. But you know? We were worse. We lived within eyesight of the trailhead for a year before we ventured there, and it took getting rid of our car completely to make it happen. And now we have become a ramshackle caravan of bikes and trailers decorated with silk flowers.

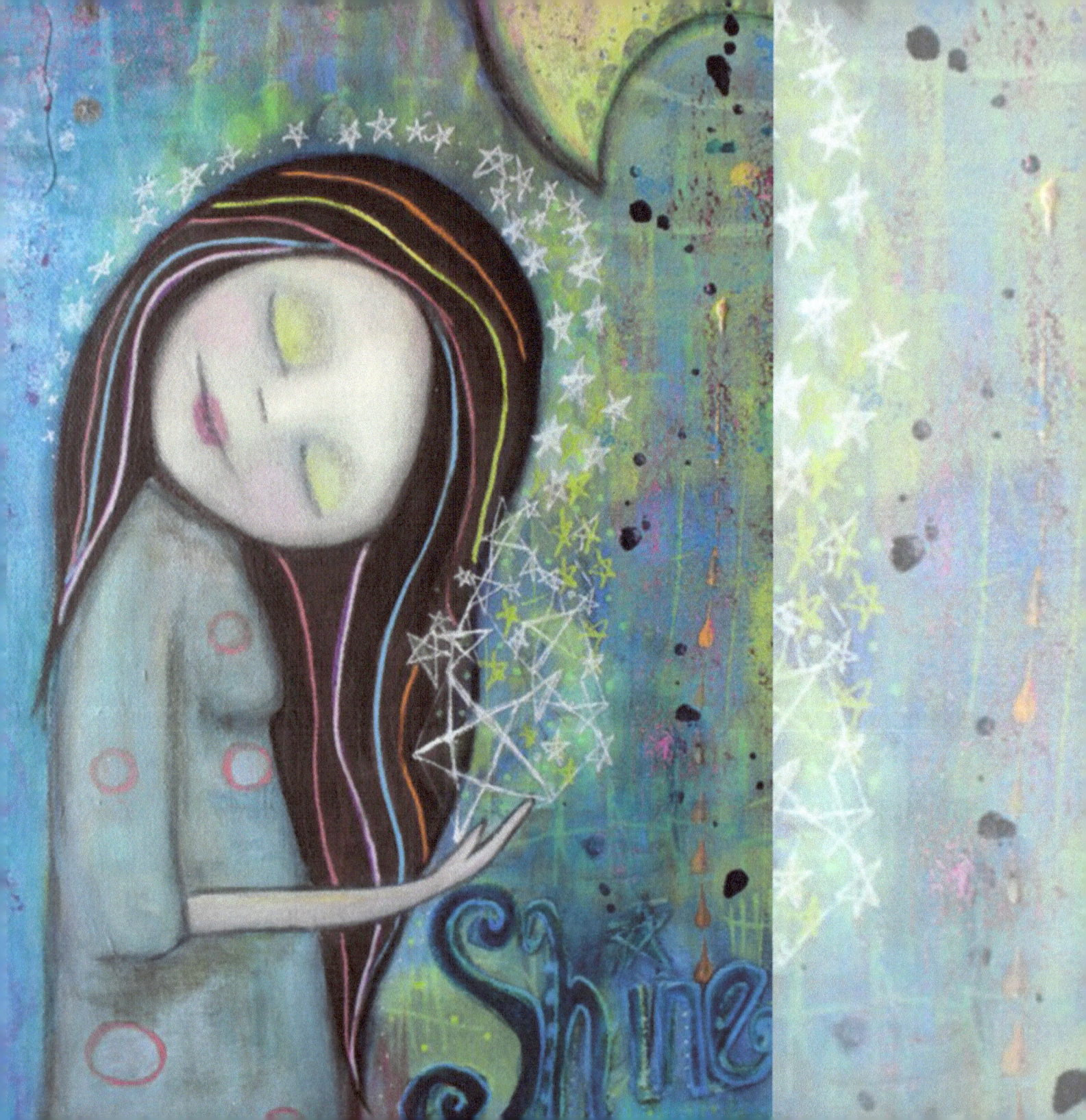

I'm grateful for garden gnomes, cuckoo clocks, climbing trees with gnarled branches, and moss.

For coffee and chai, nutmeg and cinnamon.

For citron yellow, magenta, map-water blue, chartreuse, and a bright orange shag rug in the living room.

For oatmeal, bananas, green smoothies, my husband's Magic Meals, and enchiladas.

For my kids finding fennel and chewing the stems all day like Huck Finn.

For lanterns hanging in trees.

For all the libraries I have known and loved, which became my hiding spots and my fantasy corners and the places where I built myself.

For Dolly Parton and Kenny Rogers singing "Islands in the Stream."

I'm thankful for vintage lamps. For the simple slick pleasure of freshly-brushed teeth.

I'm thankful for tall glasses of cold water and Mason jars of whiskey sipped with friends on the porch in the nighttime.

I'm thankful for the pleasure of walking aimlessly.

For thrift store velvet.

For striped socks, picture books about witches, and for snow-capped mountains I can see from certain vantage points in my neighborhood.

For the remarkable cities I have called home.

For fireflies.

For my chickens: Mary, Rhoda, Phyllis, Chamomile, Clover, and Hilda.

For stacks of books on the nightstand.

For <u>Jitterbug Perfume</u> and <u>Even Cowgirls Get the Blues</u>.

For low-watt incandescent bulbs.

For patches on old embroidered denim.

For star-printed fabric and pictures of the moon in all its phases. And I'm thankful for our wall heater that's like a fireplace and a gathering spot for our family when we hear its click-whoosh. We meet there. I'm so thankful for them—my four, my loves. And our heat, and our home, which is strung with lights

and...

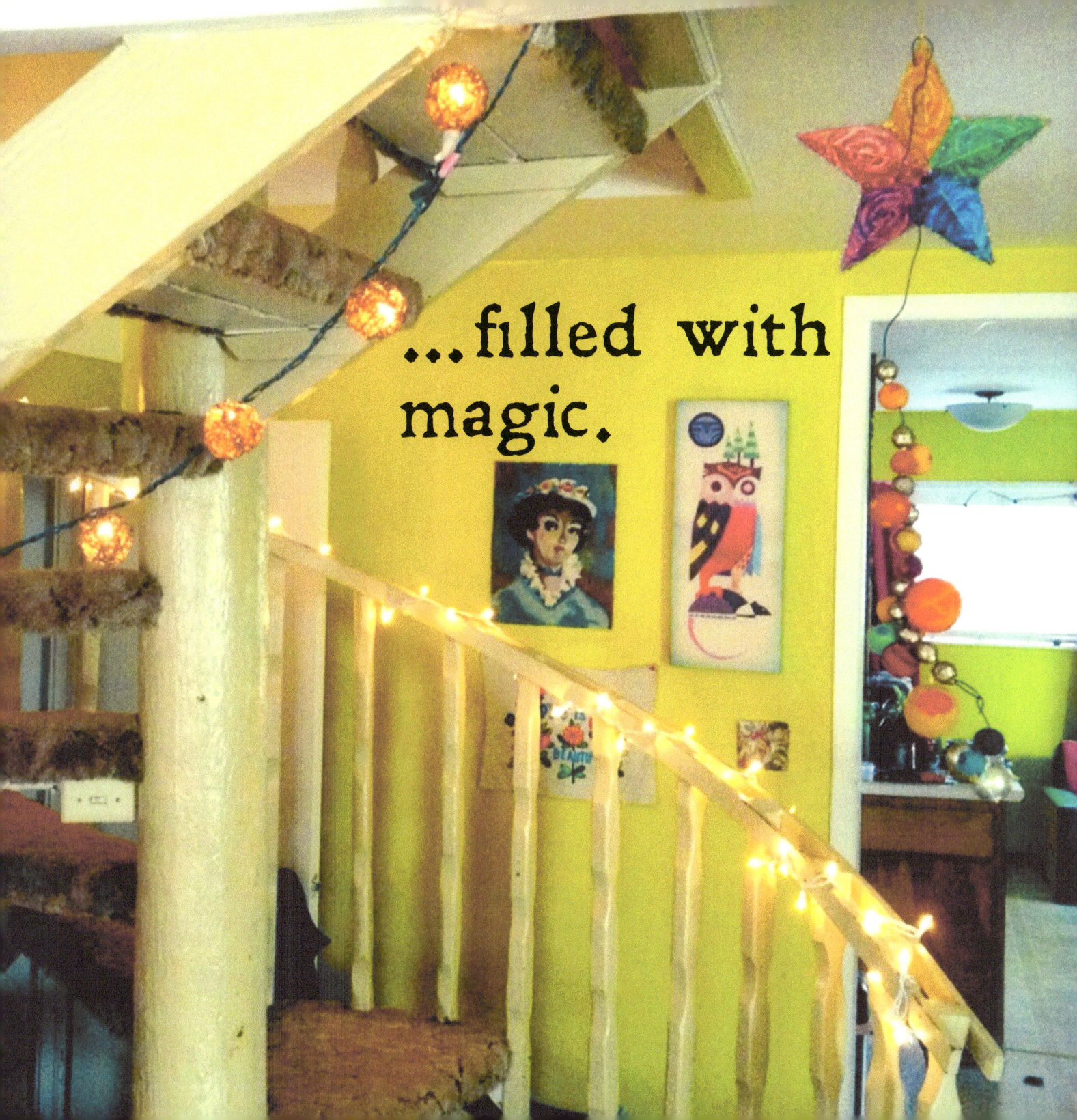

...filled with magic.

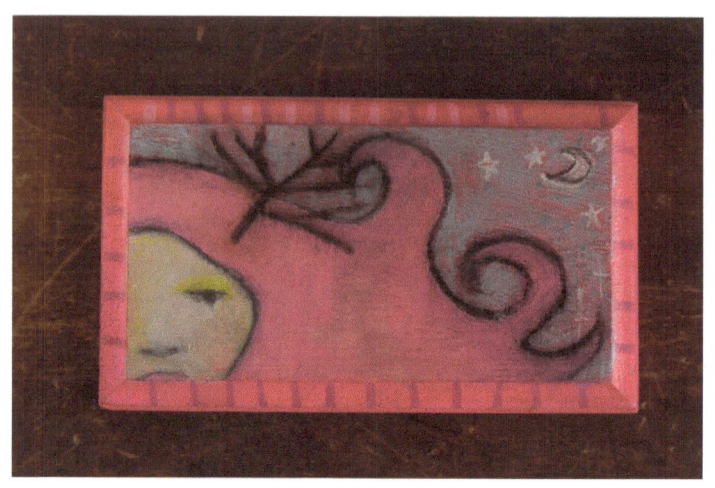

With Apologies to the Hungarian Cafe

In 1994, I would sit at the Hungarian Cafe in NYC trying so hard to kind of look like and thus BE a writer—my dream since childhood! I brought a Moleskine notebook and sat there for hours, making efforts at creating something in fits and starts, listening to the intermittent chimes from St. John the Divine Cathedral across Amsterdam Avenue. Today, almost twenty years later, I'm legitimately a paid professional writer, sitting in a jungle-themed Christian cafe in the dilapidated downtown of a third-tier suburb, listening to the dulcet tones of a couple of ten-year-old blond girls on the stage warbling "Before He Cheats" on the karaoke stage while I write about FHA loans for a mortgage company website.

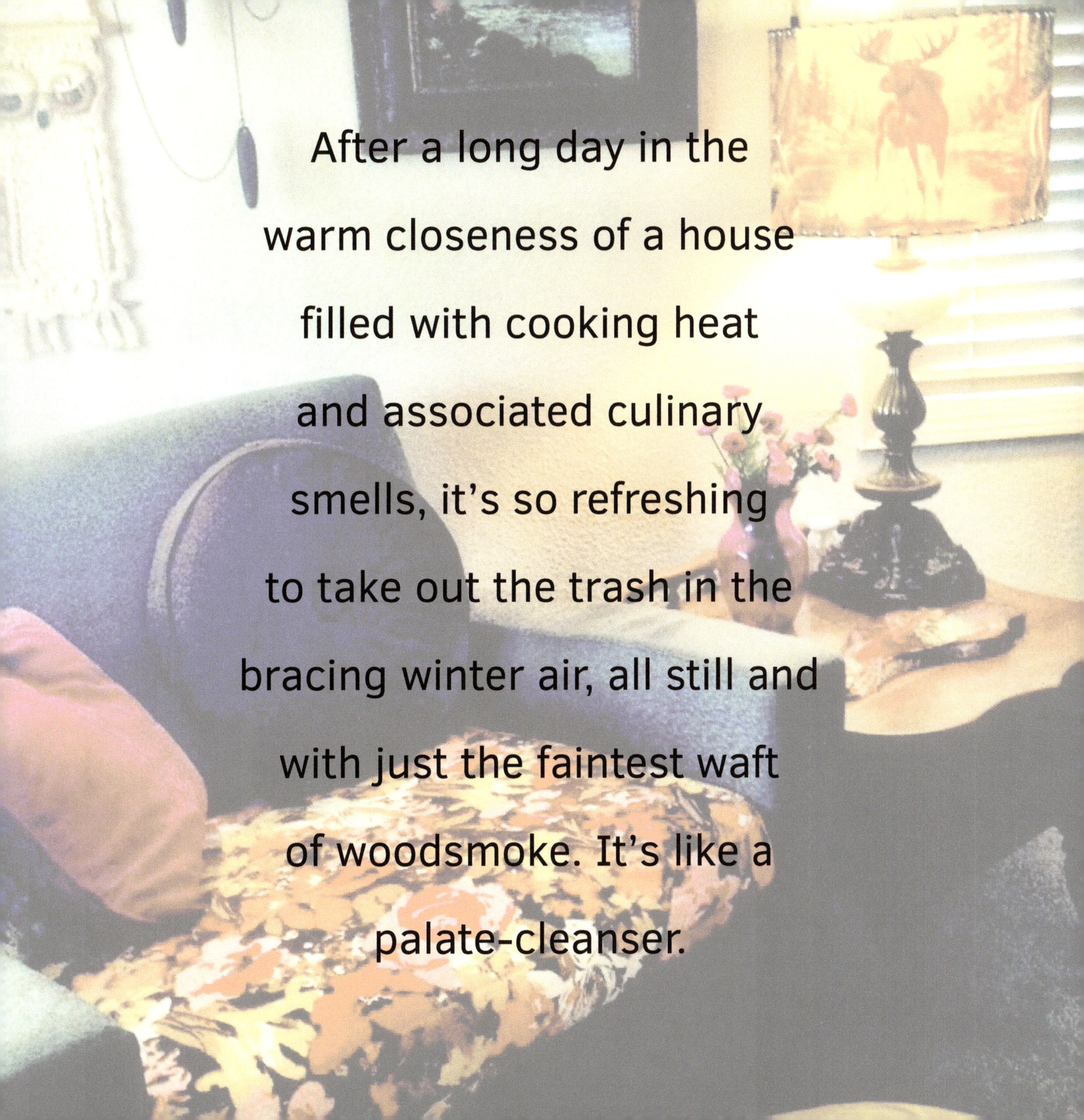

After a long day in the

warm closeness of a house

filled with cooking heat

and associated culinary

smells, it's so refreshing

to take out the trash in the

bracing winter air, all still and

with just the faintest waft

of woodsmoke. It's like a

palate-cleanser.

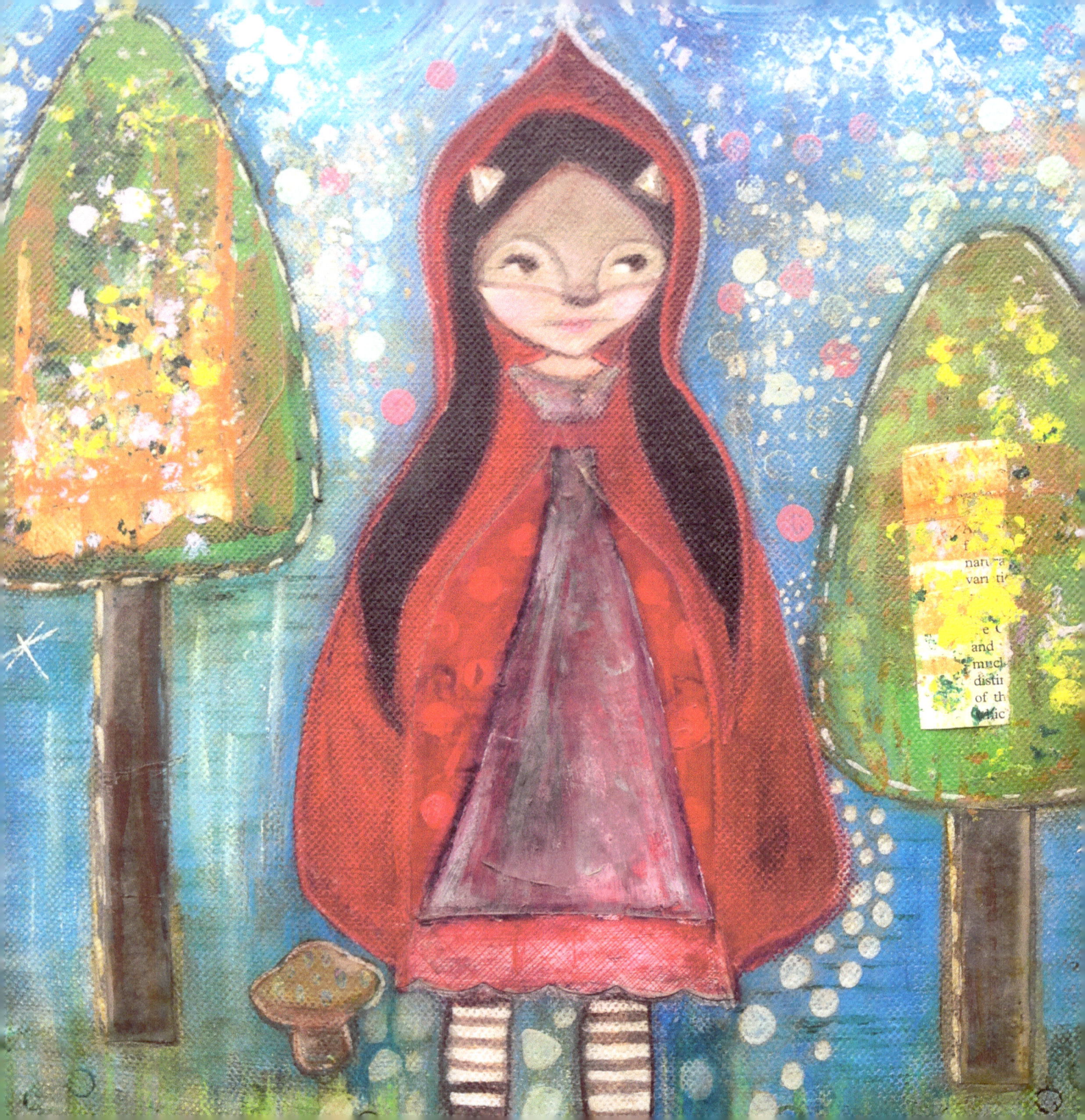

Lawton, Oklahoma

I was five. I was small, with hair as pale as milk, and I was about to become a graffiti artist. I was in Oklahoma, playing in our tidy, treeless front yard in a bare suburban neighborhood. I could come and go like that, there wasn't any need for supervision in this place.

I was avoiding the grass on that particular day, because though it was always mowed and edged, it was angry grass, bristly and spiky but nobly drought-resistant, standing stock upright without the courtesy to bend or fold much as you walked on it. It was one of those days that's so sunny everything looks as bleached as chalk. I was near the neighbors' yard, where they had a hedge that formed a small, cool dome that was the perfect size for me to crouch inside. Without much considering, I snapped a piece of a young green branch from that hedge. It hung on with the thin brown skin of itself until my small hands could work it back and forth enough to break it free.

The long walkway to the arched porch entry of our house was as bare as bone, perfect for rubbing wet green designs onto the concrete with the jagged edge of the small broken branch. Spirals, smiling faces, the word "LOVE," the only word I could write. There was a bright sharp smell as I kneeled low, the sticky feeling on my fingers, and I remember noticing all of this as I regarded my work with satisfaction. I drew small pointed hearts all around. I did this by carefully making a narrow letter V and then topping it with the outline of a person's bottom, that's how I remembered how to do it. But I made capital E's wrong for the longest time. I gave them so many horizontal lines in the middle they resembled a comb or, at the least, a many-tined fork.

. . .

There was a throat-clearing my father would make when he got home from work that meant he was going to have a Bad Night. It was almost imperceptible, but to my ears it was as insistent as that monotonous hoot the television would make when practicing for an emergency, and when he walked from the driveway it was there, and his eyes saw me but didn't see me. I'm not sure if it was the writing on the front walkway or the frantic scramble I did, saying what I needed to say, trying to scamper from his sight and his anger.

My vulnerability and fear brought a kind of red-faced rage forth from him, or maybe I was just the unwitting recipient and had no part in causing it, it was hard to tell. I was as still as a rabbit when it first senses it's being watched. It didn't matter that I didn't know why he was angry, but just that I knew that he was, and that I was first in line, and that the next set of events was as sure and reliable as the heavy roll of a pinball sliding back into its ready spot. It was too late to either mend or escape, and as always I knew that if it had maybe been a non-throat-clearing night, things would have gone much differently. When he came home in a good mood, it was like freedom. Sometimes there would be a trip to 7-11 to get Marathon bars for everyone, or he'd put on the Cream record, or the Janis Joplin one my mom loved so much. He played the stereo loud enough that it shook the

walls. When he was cheerful, he wanted all the neighbors to feel his loud, infectious joy. He was grudgingly adored. The type of person people called a "character."

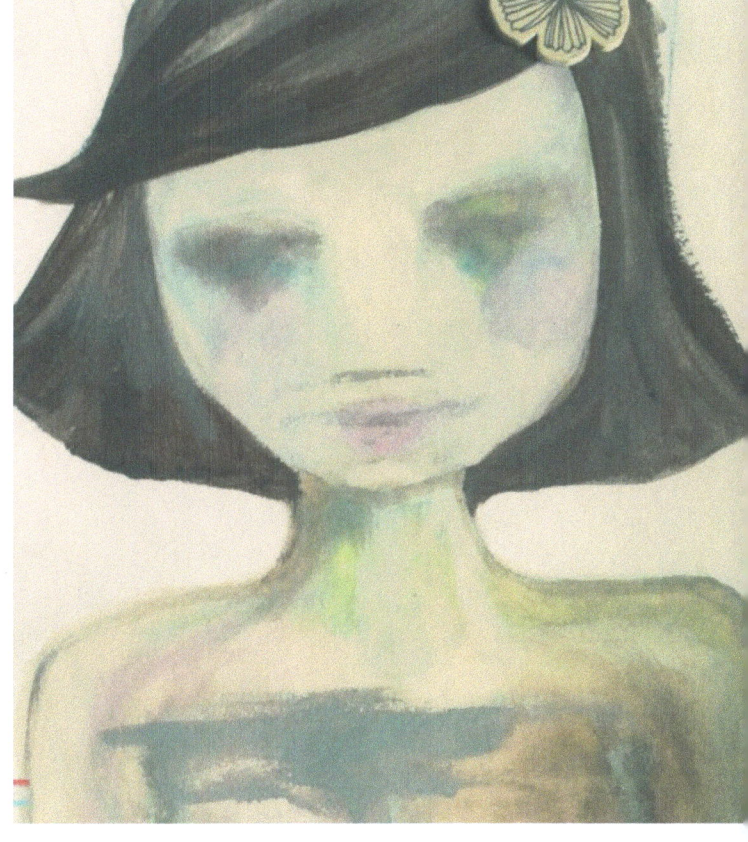

But this was not a stereo night, and there was nowhere for me to go.

I stayed as still as possible. My father's face was purple-red, and it vibrated. You could smell this kind of anger he had. He stuttered when he screamed, and repeated words. I felt far away from this place and submitted; I would

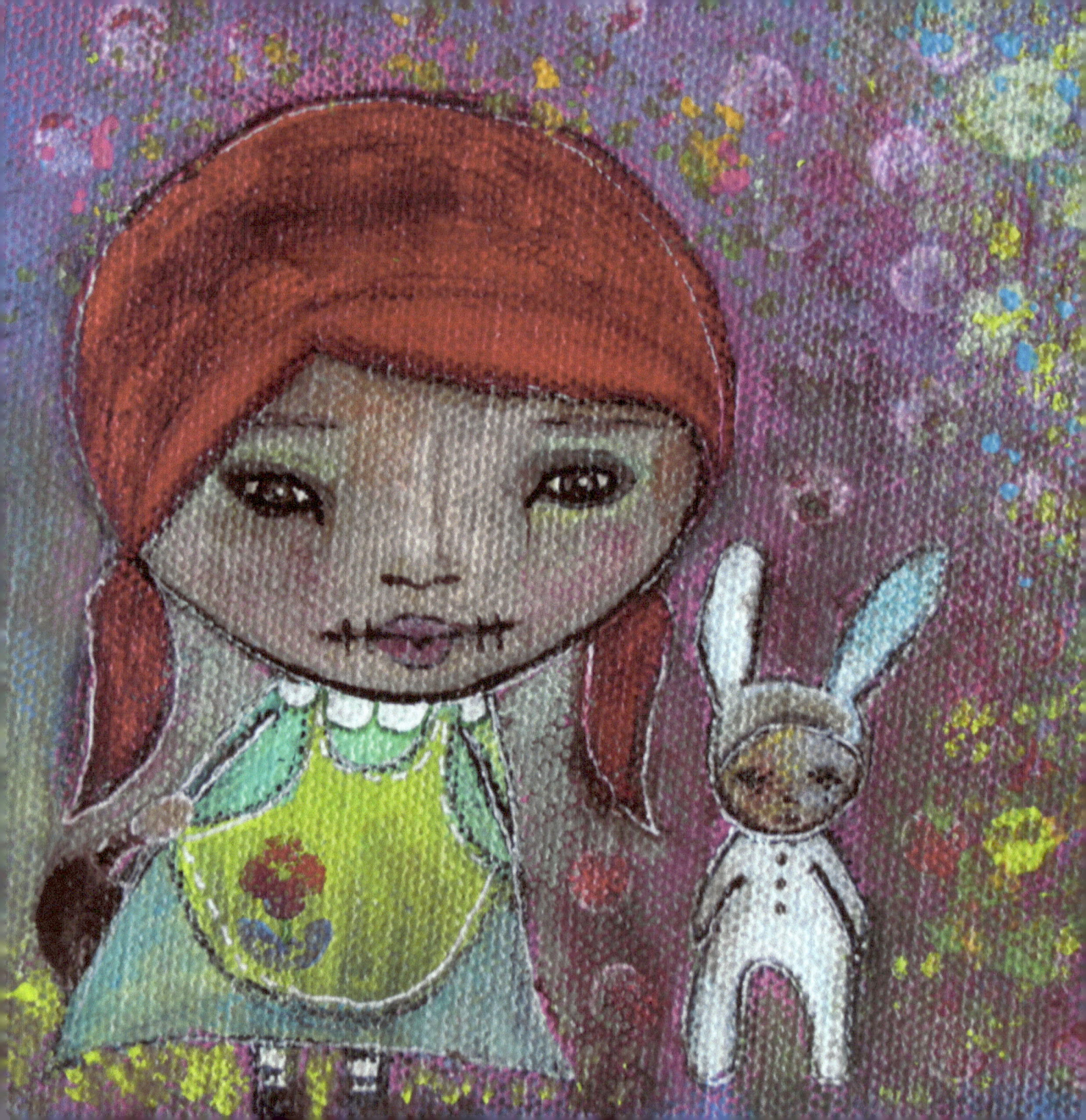

always submit. When he would spank me, it was a full-body spanking done in rage, and it was full of other things, pulling me to a place and holding my arms back. There was only this strange satisfaction that it had started and, having started, would end.

My mother could be nearby at these times, but would not hold or protect, or even provide comfort later. I remember the thin straight-across of her mouth, and the way her gray eyes seemed colorless to me. The feeling of having no one in your corner, when you are small and the person who holds such terror for you, who throws you and silences you so completely with fury, should be contrasted by one that will see your side and take it sometimes. If your mother, perhaps, would look at you with the soft eyes of an ally, and maybe back up your explanation for things, just sometimes — just once! Just once, to look into that enraged face and say "stop." Stop.

I didn't know things were different in our family, but what I did know was to fear evening time and weekends. Turning on the lights made it feel a little better, but the arrival of dusk would often find me skittering under the bed. No matter what other kids said, that wasn't where the monster was. The monster smells like Coors, and sambuca, and cigarettes. The monster is big and furious and loves you sometimes, holds you in his lap sometimes, teaches you to ride your two-wheeler on those wide treeless streets.

"O.K., now quickly look down, go ahead. Do you see that shadow? That's the shadow of a big girl riding her bike." I risked it, for just a moment, darting my eyes to the left and down. There were no training wheels on my purple big-kid's bike anymore, I could see that in the shadow. I could even see the vinyl streamers hanging limply festive from the handlebars, they were there in the shadow, too. This bike, these wide quiet streets, this sliver of father I could cling to, when it wasn't a Bad Time.

A dad's job is to teach you how swim a few strokes in the overly chlorinated neighborhood swimming pool, while your jolly baby brother crawls and bloodies his knees on the surrounding concrete, oblivious, drool and snot from nose to chest. My father's handlebar mustache would turn up at each end, you could barely see the twinkling smile under the broom of it. Sweetly: "That was all the way to the edge without any help, that was just like a fish, Corbyn Lee."

But on this day, all I wanted was to escape his view. I felt raw and unpeeled on the front walk, and kept picturing the jagged stick crayon that had started this mess — where was it now? In the after-hurting,

I was almost calmed by the lingering hitching sounds that signaled the real crying was over. There's a relief in the after-hurting, and I already knew about that at the age of five.

I had a bucket and a scrubber just the way anyone would imagine it, and I remember scrubbing the green markings off the concrete that seemed like hieroglyphs from a happier part of the afternoon. And for every day that there isn't the throat-clearing, there's a feeling of ecstatic relief that's almost like love.

Meditations On No Longer
Having a Car For My Family

Part II

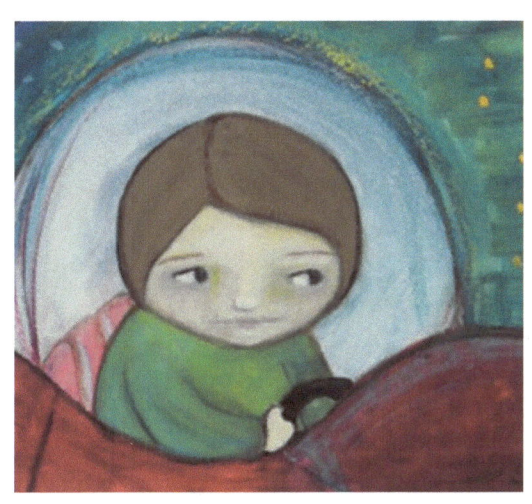

Being car-less has made our world smaller and I think that's what scares people about giving theirs up. It was certainly part of what scared me: the feeling of being trapped... but while our world has shrunk somewhat, our neighborhood has grown larger and infused with more meaning.

We've branched out farther than I initially thought we would, and distances are getting less daunting with the passing of time. We have gotten a lot better at preparing for bad weather, being efficient, packing and hauling awkward or heavy cargo, and arriving where we need to be when we need to be there. We've also gotten more accepting and gracious at being identifiable as That Crazy Biking Family, and we're more adept at putting people at ease with our decisions without making them feel ashamed of their own.

The unpredictability that our days hold doesn't scare me anymore and now I can brush the inconveniences aside with a dismissive wave. I don't flinch when I need to go to an appointment six miles away, for example. I come home when it's over and I have to remind myself, "I just rode my bike twelve miles like it was nothing." My children see the stability that comes from weathering hard times and adapting to new ways of doing things. My teenager thinks the way we're living is cool. And I'm okay with being a little bit proud of that.

I expected certain changes to be immediate, and they were: once the car was really and truly gone, we were much more discriminating about what errands were necessary. Larry and I both had had a tendency to use some quick car trip as an excuse to get away from the family for a few minutes, and find small solace in that way. I found myself mourning those late night grocery shopping trips, NPR on the radio, the windshield wipers offering contrapuntal input and just being mercifully alone in a quiet place for a little while. A quick errand by car could be a small sanity-saver for a parent of preschoolers. Of course this was amplified by the new absence of cable and Internet. Our kids have never been the kind to stare mindlessly for hours at the TV, but it was the perfect salve for those frustrating times when Larry and I and the kids were having a rough moment.

Kindergarten drop-off became a new struggle, taking all of us out of the house in the coldest part of the morning. Molly has a tendency towards orneriness, and I have found that the best way to deal with her is to utilize the element of surprise: most mornings, I pull her from bed as pink and impotent as a mewling kitten, cocoon her in a blanket, and—silently and without ceremony—dump her into the bike trailer before she has a chance to bare her fangs, even.

I didn't expect some of the other changes, though. Getting out of the driver's seat and onto the sidewalk created a more surprising shift, as potent as it is hard to explain: it was like wandering into a model railroad landscape, a diorama, something always seen from a distance. Suddenly, I was integrated into street-level life. Storefronts, parks, tables set up outside of cafes—I was right there with it, and in it. Everything looked different from this new perspective, without my high perch and tinted windows. It goes without saying that I noticed things I had missed before, like a strawberry patch growing close to the curb in

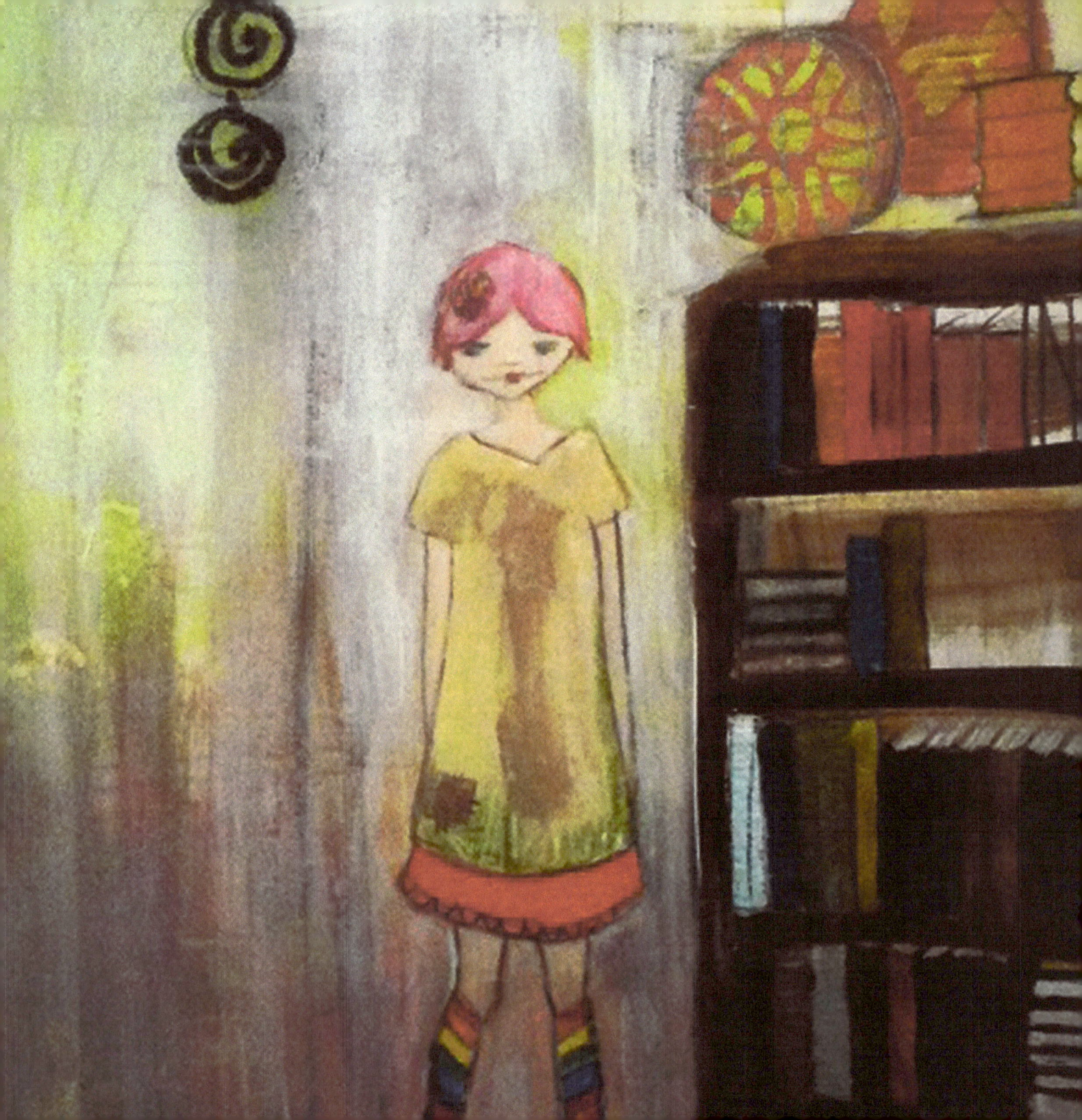

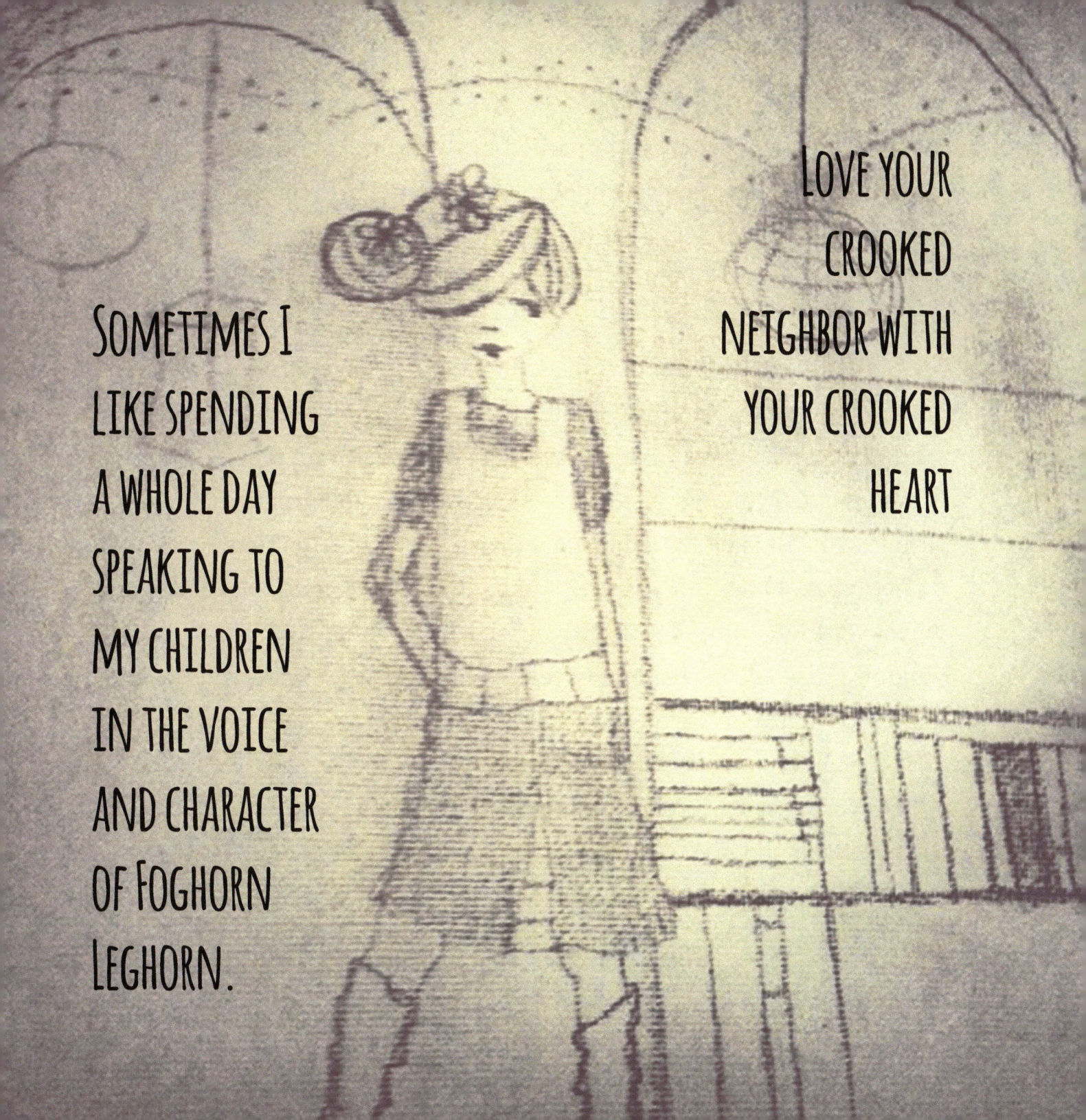

SOMETIMES I LIKE SPENDING A WHOLE DAY SPEAKING TO MY CHILDREN IN THE VOICE AND CHARACTER OF FOGHORN LEGHORN.

LOVE YOUR CROOKED NEIGHBOR WITH YOUR CROOKED HEART

a busy Goodwill parking lot: I parked the bike but kept the kids strapped in the trailer. It wasn't a safe spot for them to run around, and I knew there wouldn't be a whole lot there to pick, but like a robin hurrying to placate wide-open mouths, I plucked and delivered, plucked and delivered.

Sometimes it was good: it made me feel connected to my community to be able to wave into stores at the people we do business with: the earnest waiter at the diner whose pink smiling face always looks up at us with delighted surprise, Rose from the grocery store sitting with her back leaned against the stucco wall, smoking a cigarette on her break. Other times, I resented having to put on a social face whenever I left home. The big silver chariot with the subtly-tinted windows gave me a barrier between myself and the town around me, and I didn't have to smile when I didn't want to.

I began to notice the small differences between neighborhoods. When we crossed a certain thoroughfare and the houses got shabbier, the sidewalks did, too, with tree roots pushing fissured chunks of concrete into jagged peaks. I learned what areas were old enough that they didn't have proper curb-cuts at the corners. We discovered an old WPA-installed hopscotch grid on one nearby sidewalk, the brass numerals worn smooth with age and use. We stopped going to stores that didn't have bicycle parking racks, and frequented the places we could get to through our network of city hike-and-bike trails. Suddenly we viewed areas, thoroughfares, and shopping centers as "bike-friendly" or not. We paid attention to news reports involving cyclists hit by cars, and schooled the children about where the risks were highest.

Weirdly, we had really and truly never walked anywhere before we sold the car. We would take walks, but that was different—that was a leisurely thing, something partaken of only when it was comfortable and appealing. When something needed to get done or purchased, there was always a reason to drive, even if only a half-mile. I'm ashamed when I see now how close we live to the grocery store, and how we rationalized taking the car *every single time.* The weather was always too hot or too

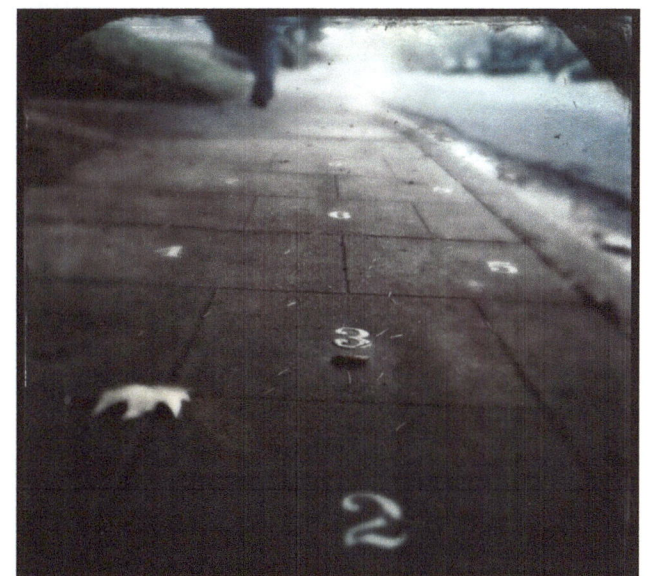

cold, or we might have concerns about how much we could carry, or we were in a hurry because of impending bedtime, a show on TV, an urge for ice cream that needed fulfillment without delay. The first evening I rode my bike to the store, I felt something close to giddiness. I called my husband: "I don't know why we never did this before! Why didn't we ever do this before?"

I had been worried about the kids' response to the huge change. I figured Zeke, at the very least, would miss the car because, well, it's a car, and motorized vehicles are pretty much his favorite thing on earth. But over these more than three years without, he rarely brings it up. When he does, though, it's impressively specific for someone so young: "Remember when we had the silver Honda Pilot?" he'll ask. Molly, true to her nature, didn't seem to notice or care. What was most surprising was Rainer's response to the change, as a young teen with all the accompanying social sensitivities: she was proud. She focused on the cool surprise of it, how dropping the information rippled impressively. She became a bellwether of eco-family living, and chose to emphasize that to others—and seemingly herself. She wore the poverty stigma lightly, like a boa around her shoulders she could easily shed.

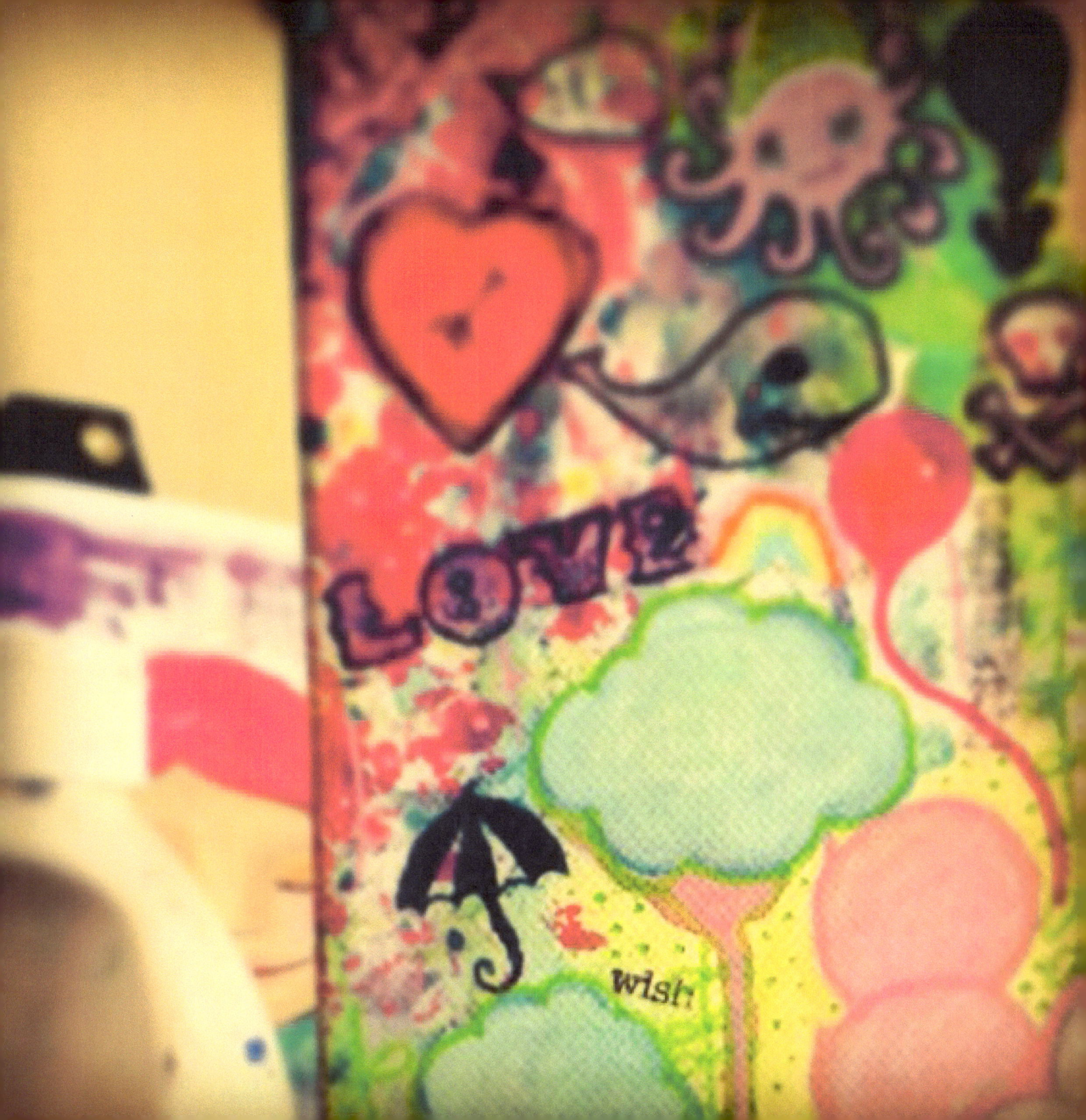

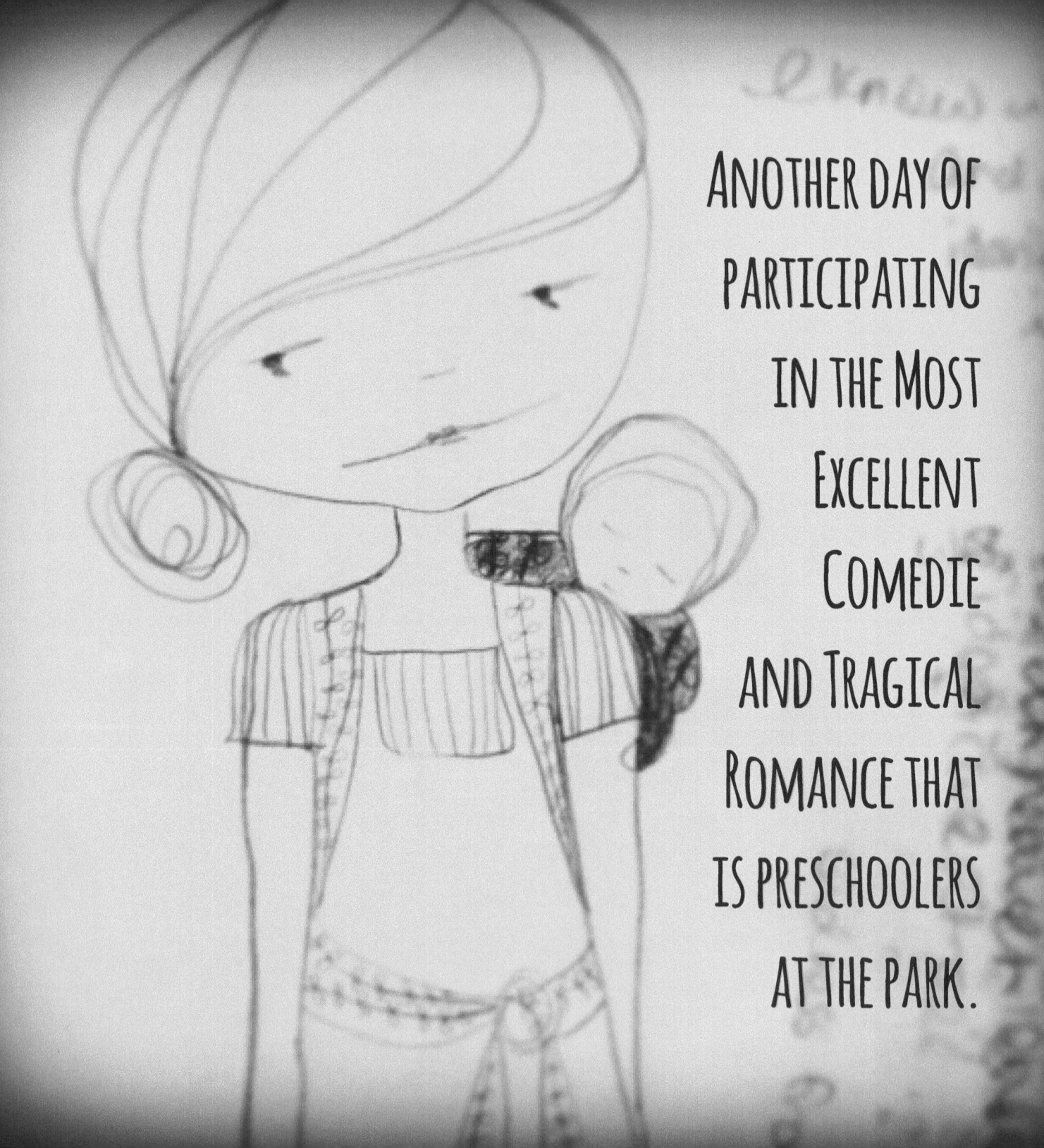

Another day of participating in the Most Excellent Comedie and Tragical Romance that is preschoolers at the park.

Indoctrinated

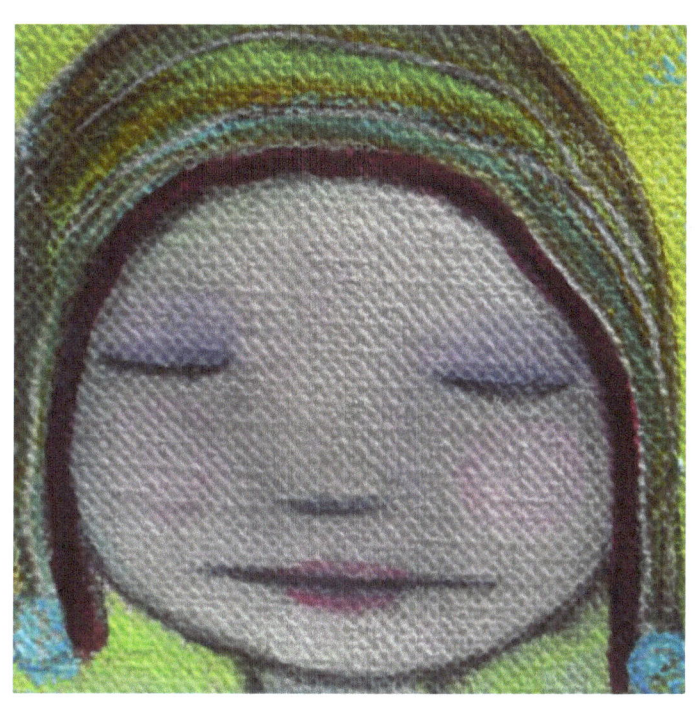

Here's how it happens: my oldest child—a preteen—is having a friend spend the night. I'm surprised how self-conscious I am on my daughter's behalf. We haven't had many guests since the recession demanded that we downsize our life, at which point we sold our only car, axed the cable and internet services, and moved into a shabby old house by the rail yard. It's really hot inside, and there's no air conditioning. Some doors don't have knobs. Our chickens have rendered the back yard unusable, and our driveway has been taken over by raised garden beds. What we lack in decorum we make up for in freedom from too many Rules About Things.

She says, "Your house is colorful."

I look at this crumbling place and I see the salvation of its under-priced square-footage and prolific fruit trees. This has been safe harbor, even with the nearby train tracks and concomitant hobos. I bite back apologetic explanations for the bicycles in the dining room and the cords from all the whirring fans that kept us from wilting in this destructive heat. We harvested pounds of squash from our garden, and that's going to comprise the bulk of our dinner. My husband steams it, seasons it lightly, and serves it with a pot of brown rice. Our young house guest eats heartily.

The next day it's just so hot, and our little neighborhood creek bubbles below the foot bridge with promise of relief. I send the older girls out, where they will break small green branches from the fennel plants that grow in great fluffy drifts on the shore. They will have to climb through the remains of a concrete ditch, make way under a bridge festooned with lovers' graffiti,

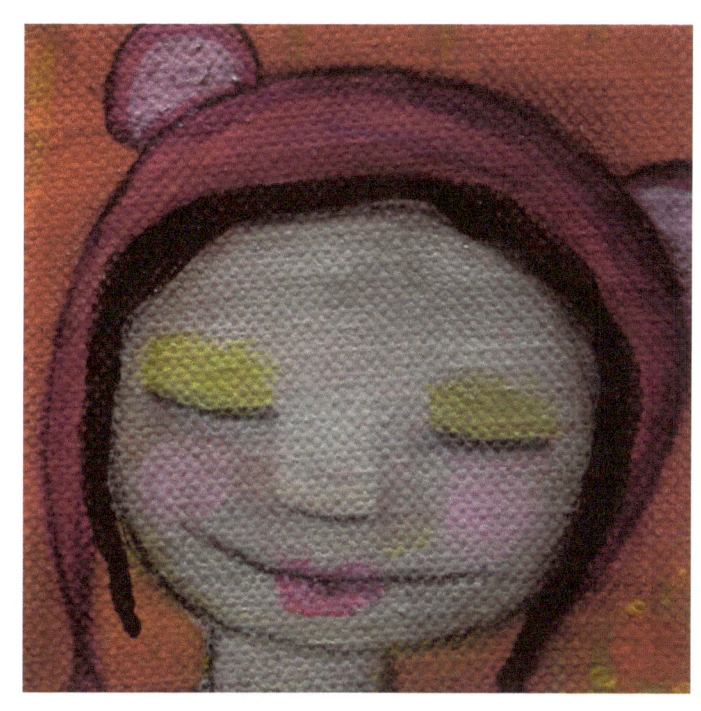

and wade through the murky water to get to the small, hidden beach made of smooth stones and small shells.

They return muddy, sun-pinked, and happy. They've collected fistfuls of fennel along with small glittering rocks and treasures. Our new friend has gotten a splinter in her foot. I make up a warm foot-bath with crushed lavender, and my son tells her that it will help with the splinter and with her emotions, too. "It'll make you feel okay until it gets better. It will give you a peaceful feeling." I smooth her hair down and kiss the top of her head, our initiate. She holds her foot up for me to investigate.

Later, I send my five-year-old to water the garden. The tomato plants have blooms, and the other plants are straining upward, not full-grown but strong, with their broad leaves facing toward the sun. Yesterday we feasted on the first truly awesome strawberries of the season, red all the way through. We tried to appreciate each strawberry for how it's slightly different from the rest. The way the sparkling flavor and seeds make them taste almost carbonated, like a festival, a

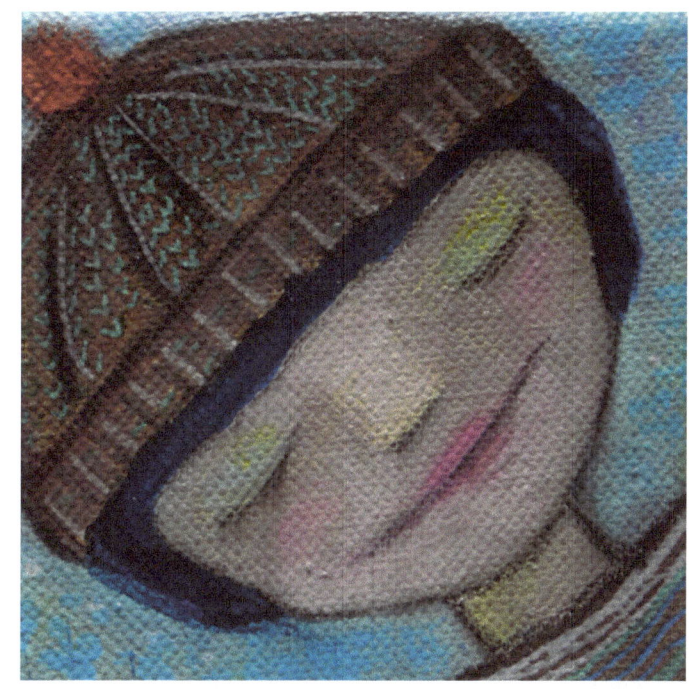

joyous clarion heralding the long sunny days. My children will have a summer of these simple memories, ones in which I participate, and others where my only job is to remove the splinters and wash off the mud upon their return.

Pick It Up and Shift It Towards the Light

I didn't get published as a writer until I turned forty, because my parents likened it as less of a career path and more like attempting to become a Hollywood ingenue. So I packed it away and once in awhile, I'd have an opportunity to whip it out like a parlor trick. When attempting to charm someone via email, or in the writing of letters of any sort.

So here's how it started: we decided to sell our only vehicle in order to pay the rent. An editor friend who, at the time, was working for a website chronicling the realities of the New Economy, wanted me to write about how we were surviving without a car as a suburban family of five. He wanted me to report on our family's experience living with financial devastation. About the choices we made, and the prices we paid for those.

Which brings me to: *carlessness*. My word processing program doesn't want to even acknowledge it's a word; it's just a snippet of the zeitgeist and that takes longer to integrate. It's too close to carelessness, and maybe that resemblance is a bad thing. You see, outside of places like New York City and maybe Portland, not having a car–especially when you are the suburban mother of three–is a sign and symbol of having Blown It Big Time. But we are without a car. It was an easy decision when we made it: we couldn't pay the rent, and we had gotten rid of, sold, and downgraded everywhere we could. What we had was a paid-for, valuable hunk of metal parked in the driveway and a roof we preferred to keep over our heads. Some people make another choice: to move in with family, perhaps. "Temporarily," of course. But it was no accident that we had found ourselves in Northern California, far away from both of our parents' households in Texas. We had severed the ropes of that safety net and had no regrets. You see, there are some sorts of "safety" that are so fraught with danger and damage that calling upon them would prove more harmful than beneficial.

So we carried on, working what jobs we were able to get, and trying to shake money from trees. We take our children on errands in our bike trailers, pedaling in the sweltering heat or in downpours, faces held in caricature expressions of grim determination. It's been an adventure. A noble experiment. So many others around us are in similar straits, so this whole thing–newfound poverty–has an air of camaraderie to it, and

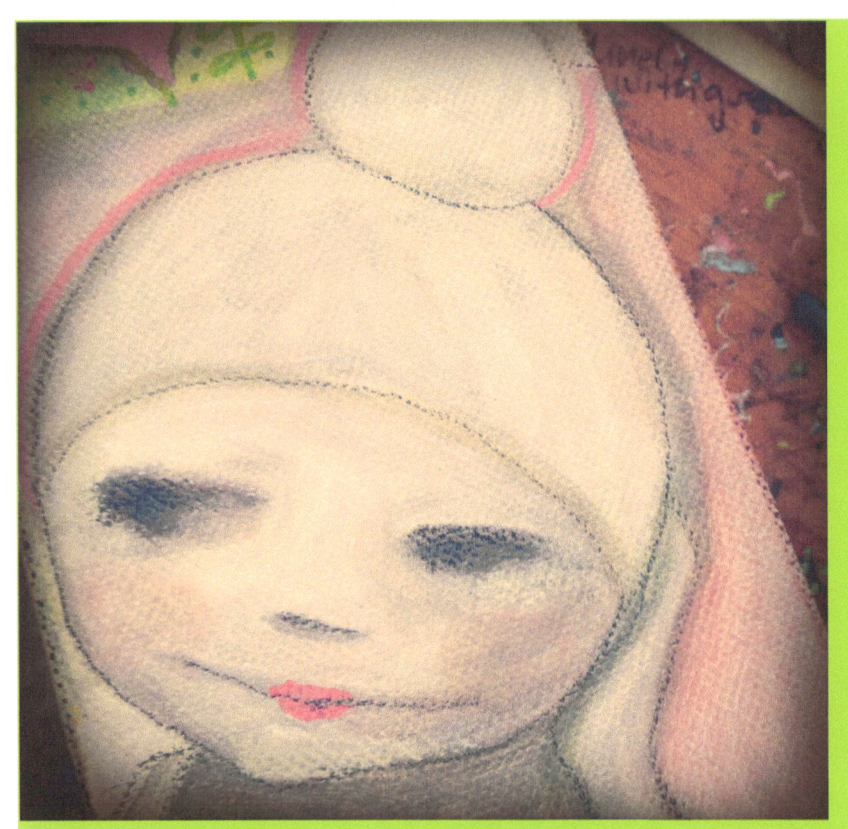

WHEN I LIVED IN GRASS VALLEY (AMONGST THE DREADLOCK'D,) I WAS FRIENDLY WITH AN ODD YOUNG WOMAN NAMED AMIE. SHE LIVED IN A SHACK MADE OUT OF RECLAIMED BARN PLANKS IN A DANDELION-COVERED VALLEY WITH HER DAUGHTER, TIGER LILY. SHE WASHED THEIR DISHES IN THE CREEK, AND COOKED ON A POT-BELLY IRON STOVE. SHE STOOD WITH HER ARMS TIGHTLY FOLDED IN FRONT OF HER. CHAIN-SMOKED UNAPOLOGETICALLY. HI, AMIE, WHEREVER YOU ARE. YOU WERE A STRANGE BEAUTY. I FIND MYSELF MISSING YOU TODAY.

whole new ways of doing things have taken root. It was cool at first--
it was novel to us, and we felt we were part of a larger social upheaval
that had a lot of beauty hidden within. We've done it all: bartered, gotten
backyard chickens, grown a vegetable garden. Over the last few years,
I've written so many essays about the New Simplicity that I started
to sourly dismiss it as "Chicken Soup for the Recessionista's Soul,"
and even after writing an entire (unpublished, for real and persuasive
reasons, trust me) memoir about it, I couldn't wash my hands of it soon
enough. I'm no one to emulate. I make every bad decision there is. I'm
AWESOME at one thing: snatching defeat from the jaws of victory.
(Working on fixing that one, though.)

I look at my children and I want to say, *I'm sorry, I'm sorry you're
having to wear this need and pretend it's okay,* I'm sorry there are no
birthdays at pizza parlors or dance lessons. I'm sorry I can't send you
with a handful of change that I don't have so you can get a candy bar at
the corner store. I'm sorry you notice what other families enjoy—simple
things, a drive to the country, being able to see the Pacific Ocean for
once (just once, for chrissakes, it's just two hours away!) or a weekend
of camping—and you notice the difference and have to ask me why. I'm
so sorry I cannot provide for you the things that were provided for me.

I'm sorry that a simple trip to the doctor to check for pinkeye or an ear infection has to be a negotiation based on the twenty bucks in co-pay expense versus what may be curable through the healing tendencies of time and the body's own resources.

I wear bright pink lipstick (cheap knock-off brands, one tube a year) and have my cruiser bike decorated like a parade float. I let my children dress with colorful abandon. We played by the rules and we lost everything that offered us safety and security, so to hell with the rules, I teach them. You will get screwed-over six ways to Sunday, so find the hidden magic, I say. Do you see that smooth brown stone? Pick it up and shift it towards the light, and you will see small bits of glitter like tiny stars. I try to tout this lifestyle as one we would have chosen back when we were flush with income and silly material wants, and absolutely yes . . . there are lessons we've learned. We can be a band of vagabond raconteurs in satin and velvet castoffs, carrying torn parasols with glued-on pompom trim . . . and yes, there are blackberries that grow wild all over this town. So much beauty in debris and detritus.

But I'm tired and tearful. This last blow—the foundation that hired me to fight human trafficking and ended up defrauding me of five weeks' pay and my future with them—shook me to my core. I was thoroughly convinced I was making a decision that would pull us out of this world of bulk starches and scratchy blankets. Instead? Yet another setback.

Larry and I have a marriage where our struggles manifest themselves in silent regret and disappointment (and a lot of space between us in our marital bed) versus thrown fists or dangerous addictions. But no amount of pharmaceuticals can prop me up forever, and it's I who have to keep this creaky ship with its patchwork sails afloat. I'm sure it's this lifelong sense of entitlement that has probably contributed to my lack of ability to turn things around and make something from nothing. Why? Why do I have such a loathsome baked-in trait? I wasn't spoiled as a child. I'm forty-three years old. I have been the primary breadwinner for most of our marital alliance; I know how to do this. I am not imbecilic. What's wrong with me? I have three children. With my strong legs and my sturdy bike I pull them where they need to go. I look at my husband while we sit on the porch at night and listen to the soothing rumble of the nearby passing trains.

The hand I reach out to him is conciliatory. Apologetic.

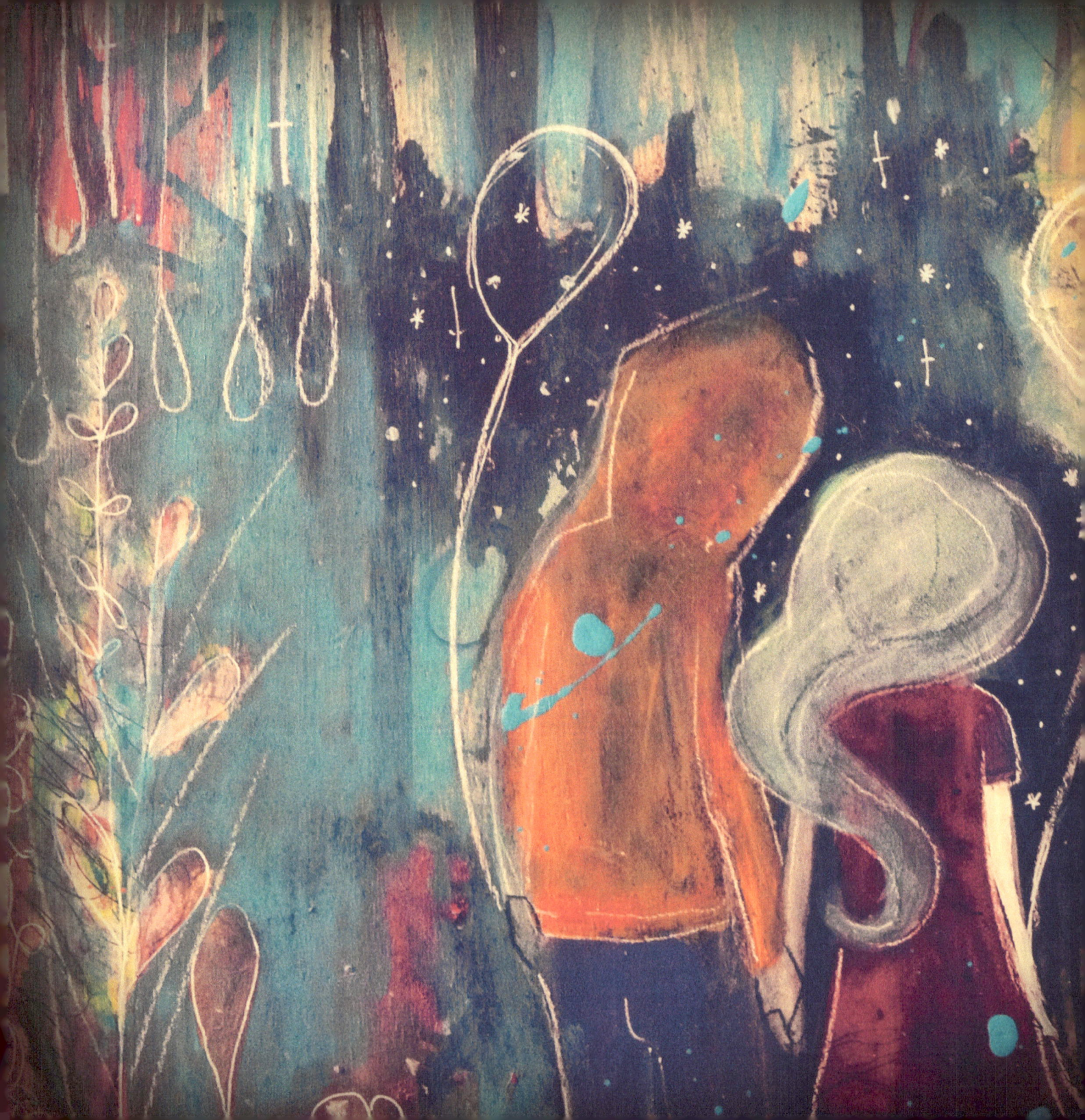

Meditations On No Longer
Having a Car For My Family

Part III

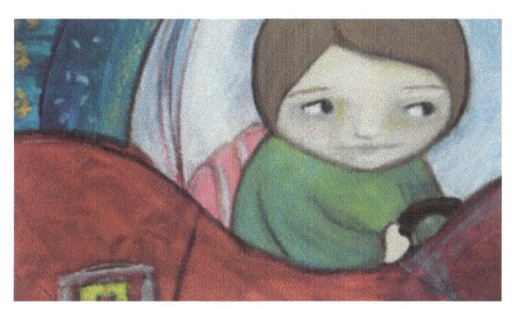

Even with all reassuring evidence to the contrary, I still worried about the kids' reaction to not having a car and having to get everywhere on foot, bicycle, or bus. In trying to make up for these changes, I think I still go out of my way to try to make things fun. There is no limit on how loud we can play the radio at home. There is a rollicking quality to getting around the way we do: we stop for wishing wells, we take breaks when we intercept the ice cream truck, and we have been known to tote home a menagerie of broken Happy Meal toys if we pass a bin of them at the thrift store. It's a scrappy childhood for them, one with more unpredictability and unplanned days than we had in the past.

Getting lost is altogether different when you're not in a car. It becomes a burden of magnitude, involving weather considerations and the needs for food, water, and bathrooms. Simple miscalculations can mean a seemingly endless trek through inhospitable territory. Rail yards. Industrial areas with corrugated metal warehouses. Setting off for a day of errands means making a plan, and I'm not just talking about remembering bottled water and bananas. I also have to figure out in what order to do things: should we pick up the parcel at the post office and then circle around to the other part of town for the groceries? How big is the parcel? Will it fit into our shopping cart? Cars become giant traveling purses, way stations, and a safe "home base" in the life of a family. A poorly-charted course might become, in a car, a meandering adventure wherein the kids fall asleep in their car seats and nothing is really lost but time and gasoline, but on a bike, that scenario becomes potentially perilous. When we got home from one early-on gargantuan misfire in which I got us hopelessly lost in over ninety-degree weather, seven miles and two hours later we listlessly fell into the house and lay still, while my husband fretted and brought the kids and me water and cold wash cloths. I could feel my heart beating in my cheeks.

Days like that were part of the steep learning curve that we climbed when we became car-free, but it's gotten worlds better as we have become much more safe and savvy. We call on resources when we're

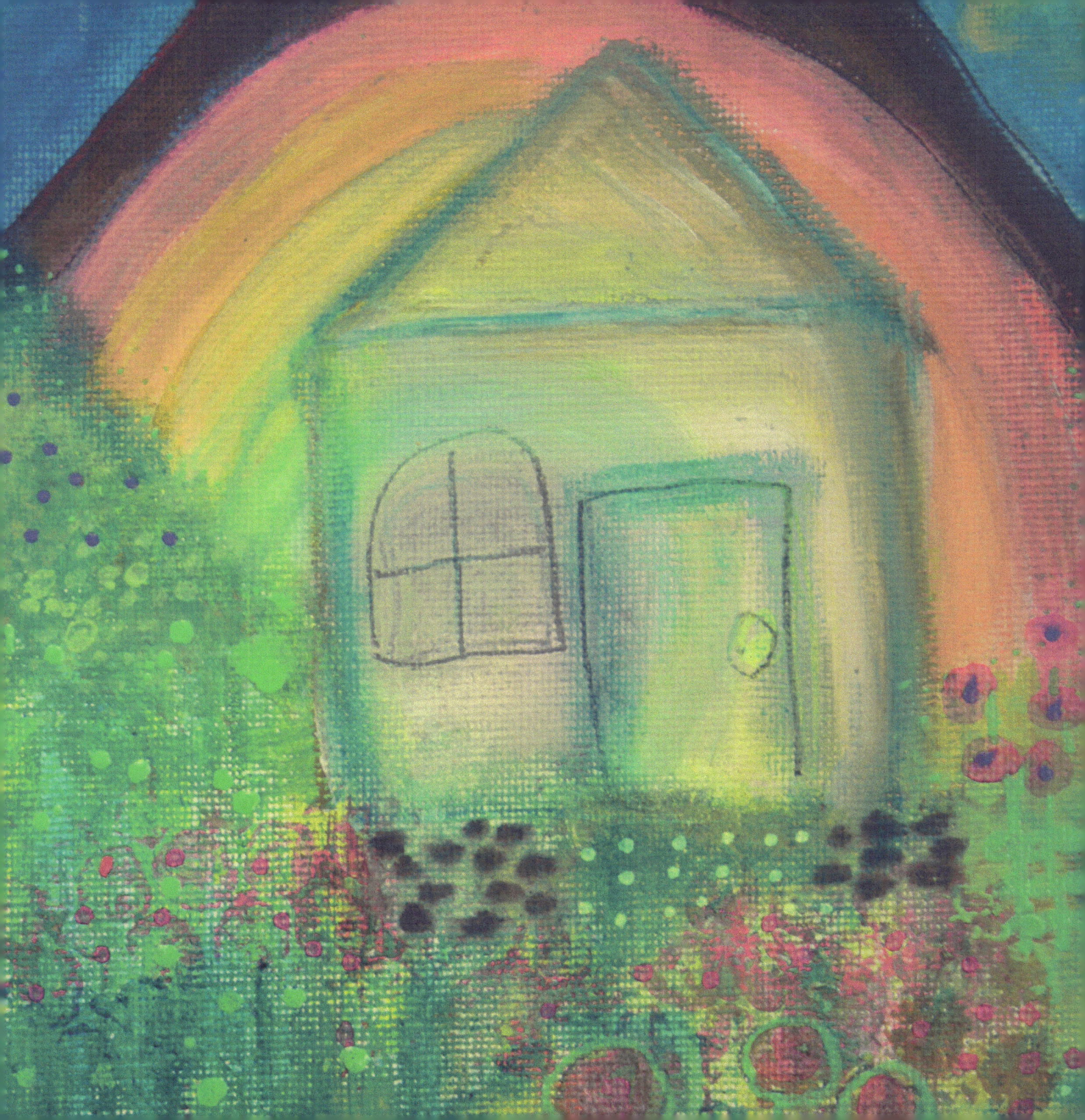

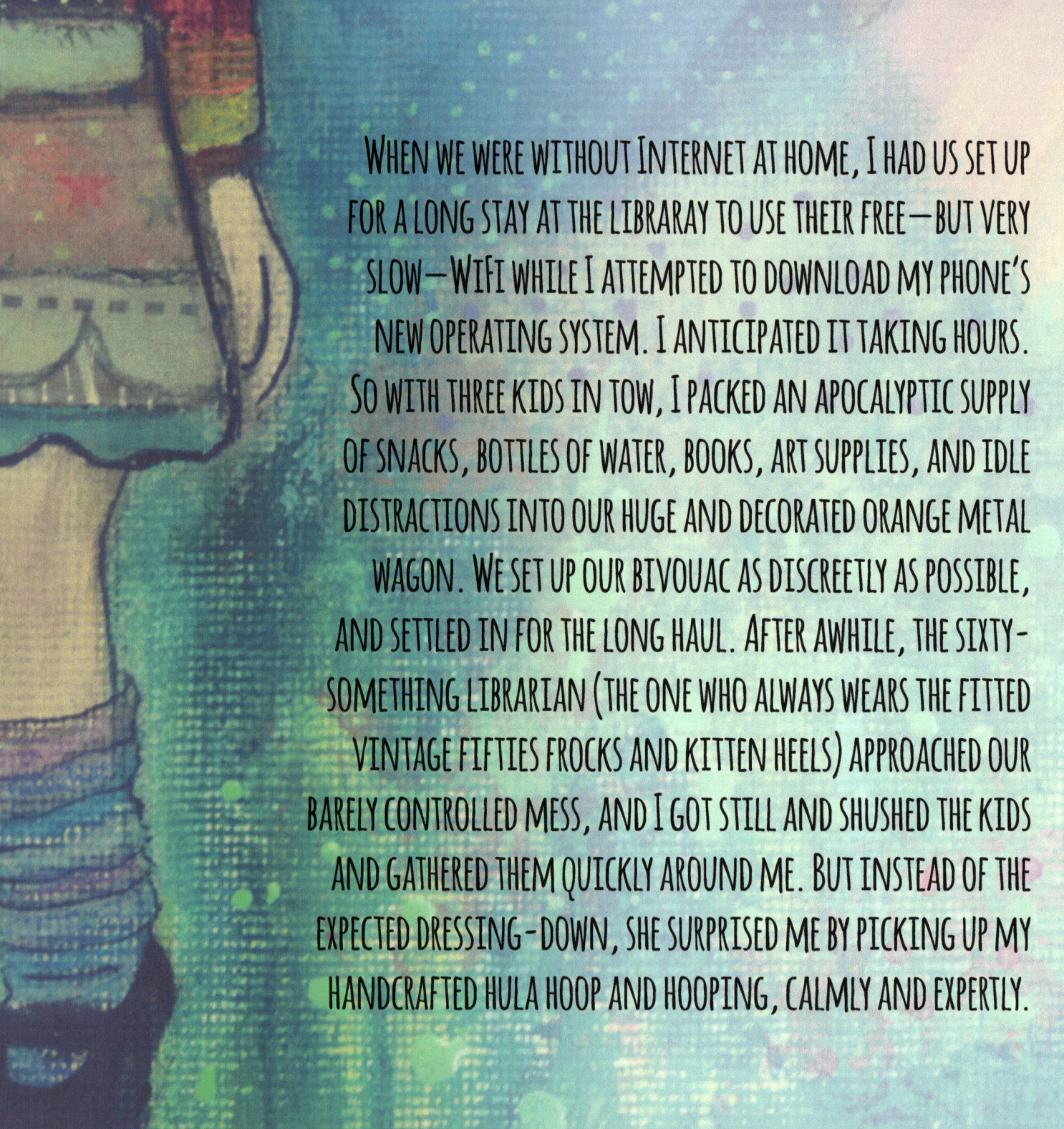

When we were without Internet at home, I had us set up for a long stay at the libraray to use their free—but very slow—WiFi while I attempted to download my phone's new operating system. I anticipated it taking hours. So with three kids in tow, I packed an apocalyptic supply of snacks, bottles of water, books, art supplies, and idle distractions into our huge and decorated orange metal wagon. We set up our bivouac as discreetly as possible, and settled in for the long haul. After awhile, the sixty-something librarian (the one who always wears the fitted vintage fifties frocks and kitten heels) approached our barely controlled mess, and I got still and shushed the kids and gathered them quickly around me. But instead of the expected dressing-down, she surprised me by picking up my handcrafted hula hoop and hooping, calmly and expertly.

in a lurch, but that's rare. Sometimes when the unpredictable truly does happen—like wind that actually threatens to lift the trailers aloft like hot air balloons with the children looking down, startled . . . or when the sky opens up with that sort of rain and thunderstorm where everything goes sort of green and the hairs raise on your arms with each flash of electricity—we just stop and take cover wherever we are. We've ridden in rain, wind, cold, and heat again and again. I have learned to be okay with being the family that bursts into a store during a downpour and takes shelter—for hours, sometimes. We try to be charming; it buys you a lot of tolerance when you're sitting on the floor killing time at Target. We've become so much better at establishing our limits. In a car, you can see your fuel tank creeping its way to "empty," or that your "check engine" light has come on. It's not as clear when you're looking at the glassy eyes of a five-year-old and wondering how long she really can go before we make it to the next destination. My kids carry heavy stuff if I need them to, and walk really far. We sit on curbs and wait for buses or fix flat bike tires. Sometimes we get stuck somewhere until someone can help us.

But someone always does.

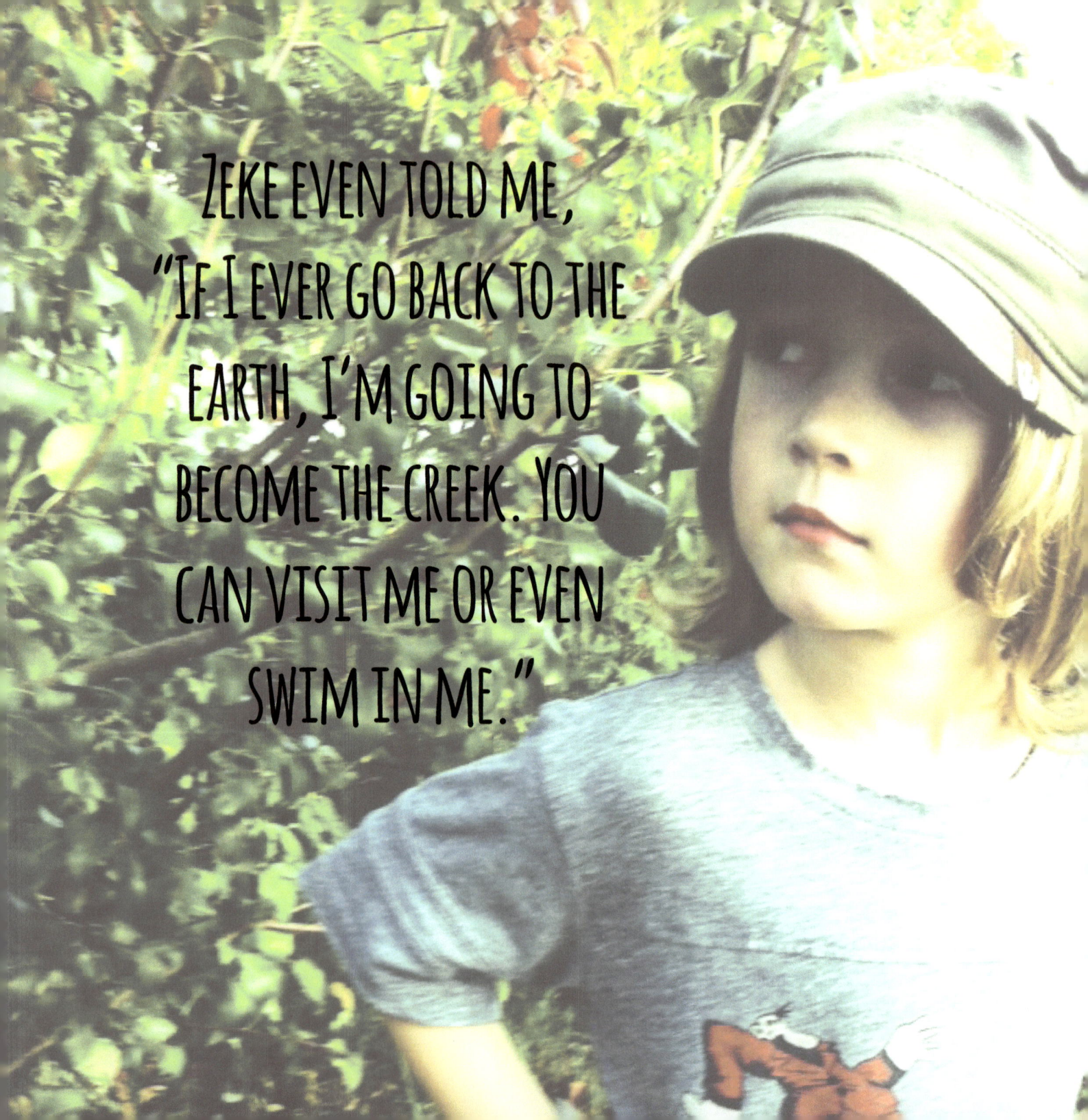

Zeke even told me, "If I ever go back to the earth, I'm going to become the creek. You can visit me or even swim in me."

My Summer Ghost

A ghost spent some time with me this summer, and he lived in my computer. He knew my name, where I had lived in 1972, where my pain had begun. My Cherokee grandmother had warned me of this type of ghost, in her way. She had a saying, something like, "there are three types of friends. Those that are there for a reason. Those that are there for a season. Those that are there forever. Two out of those three will leave you before you're ready."

This man—my ghost—had skin brown as the good dark soil you never find in Oklahoma, where the dirt is red. Legend says the dirt is red in Oklahoma due to all the blood that had been shed there. That is where my pain started, in my home... and where his started, too... my ghost. He came up on my screen and he said "I knew you, little girl. I knew you when you were being hurt and started feeling very afraid of home, because I was the little black boy down the street whose father killed a man in our living room. My stepfather raped me throughout my childhood. I'm here to show you the path to climbing out and away."

He had dreadlocks and wore a Buffalo Soldier hat his great-grandfather had kept, long stored, he told me, a source of pain that he reclaimed and wore with defiance. He smiled at me lovingly, and with a facial expression that held both pity and understanding. He told me the tears could keep coming if they needed to but they would have to stop sometime if I was going to be strong. If I was going to shed this baggage, this weight I carry around, if I was to be a Queen. He told me he had never spent a lot of time crying—and that really he never had—but that he got into a lot of trouble, instead, in the years after escaped from his abuser.

I told him that I always cry when I'm angry.

And right then, in spite of his claims mere moments ago, I saw my ghost cry for the first and last time. And in a voice I could barely understand, he stopped and said, "I spent a lot of time breaking kneecaps for you, girl."

He put his strong hand to his forehead

and his chest shook. I cried and touched the screen impulsively and told him I wish we could have helped each other back then, grasped small hands, black and white, and run far and fast across the tarantulas and bleached-white sidewalks, across the dry spiky grass, but to where? The farthest I went was on my yellow metal tricycle, riding slowly, steadily, along the long straight ribbon of concrete. How far can I go. How far can I go. My ghost went far. He went to prison, eventually... for fighting, drinking, and drugging his way out of this pain. Now he works for the poor and in need, around the world. He's an innovator, a change-maker, raising people up with his strong hands. Spreading love and charity after a lifetime of pain and anguish.

When I started repeating self-defeating things about myself, how the things that had happened had turned me into a bad person, too, he'd get up from his chair and sort of hunch his back and just start singing this kind of crazy scat until I'd shut up. He'd ask, "are you quite done?" For as long as I can remember, as an adult, I felt like if I were asked to paint a self-portrait—the internal kind, how I see myself, not the mirror's lie—I'd see a well-muscled black man with a snarl and tattoos, one whose fists are clenched and whose face challenges you to just Go Ahead, Try. That's who I call on when I need

that feeling of invincibility, like none of it ever happened, the red dirt, the years of unpredictable anger and violence, of being afraid

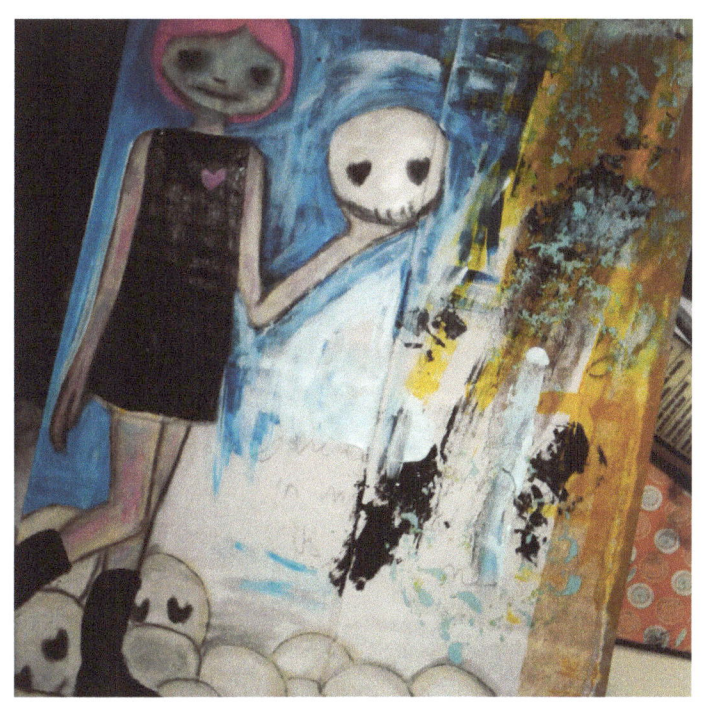

of your own parents, of your own home, the feeling of having no place that was safe. And in short time this summer, my ghost became my safety. A text of "today is going to be a great day for you. You are stronger than what happened. I love you. R." And that was like a sweet guitar strum in my ear, and my eyes would close and my head tilt with an almost drunken feeling of peace, just with those words. Because my ghost was there. He knew Everything. I could rewrite every hurt with his strong arms around me. I could paint a whole new painting, one where I didn't hide behind bushes and under beds, where I didn't cut huge bleeding sections out of the bottoms of my feet where no one would see, but where I could march, add to the red dirt, add to the red dirt. I sliced these giant swathes of flesh off my feet for years, and at night I would have to peel off my blood-soaked socks and throw them away. My mother had to wonder what was happening to all my socks. Periodically, I'd find new replacements—the kind that came in multiples, in a bag—laid on my bed without comment.

And there came a day when I wasn't

ready and he wasn't there, and it was if we had never met. All contact ceased. A DVD of a favorite movie I had sent to him came back marked "Undeliverable." And the crying came back, and it came back harder than ever, because I wasn't ready, and I thought maybe it was time, finally time for the hospital, that I had created my fantasy healer, someone who could make it all better, and I still don't know if that's not true. When I try to contact him now, he responds as if we've never met or doesn't respond at all. That's the thing about ghosts. They're damned unreliable.

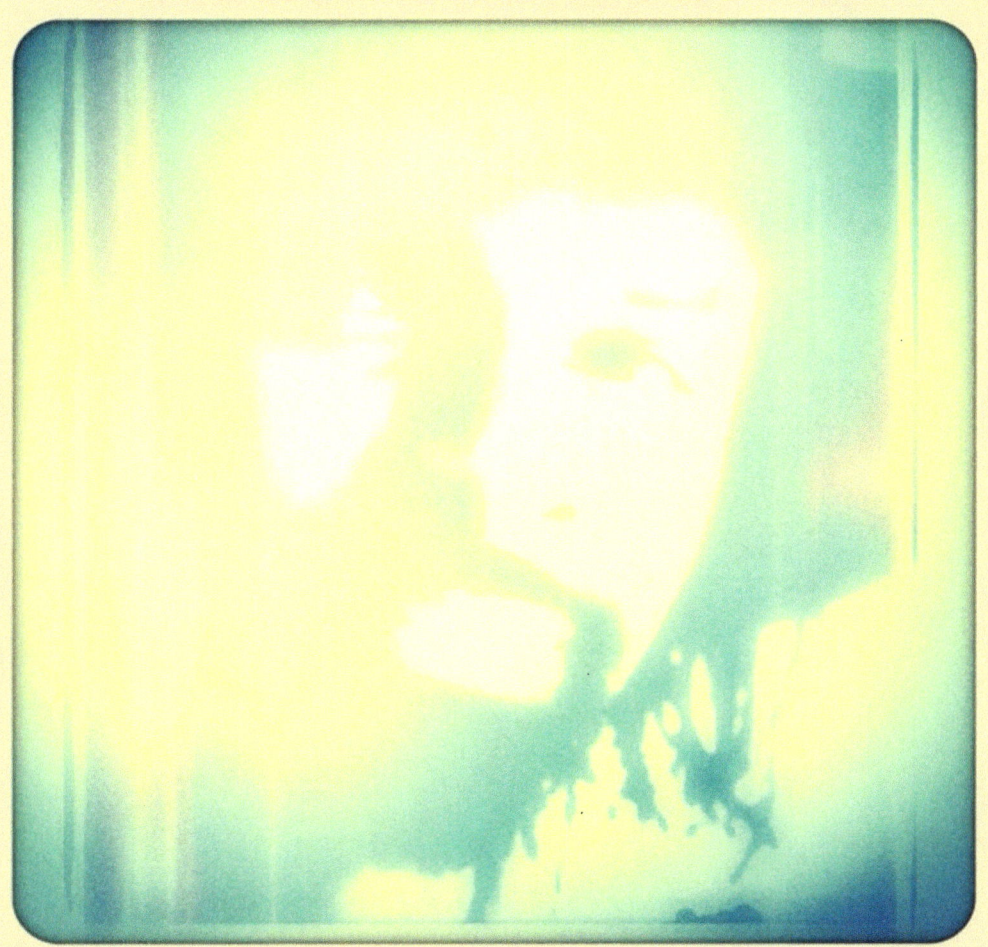

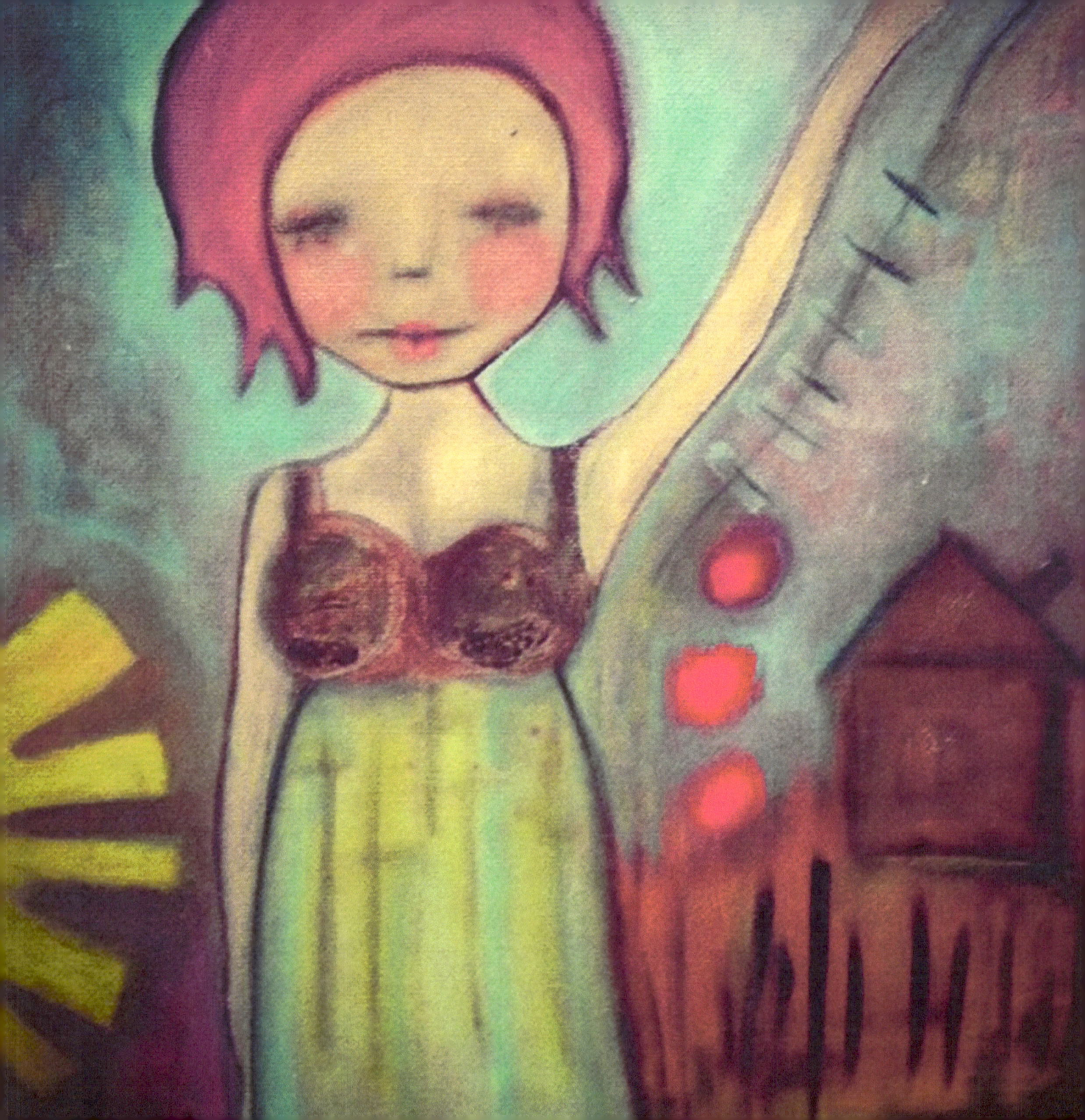

A friend of mine who is in medical school informs me that if you compare a strand of human collagen and a steel cable of equal diameter, the collagen strand is actually stronger. However, I counter that it takes only SEVEN POUNDS of pressure to break your collarbone. And consuming a bottle of Vicodin * as prescribed * will completely inhibit your ability to poop for an entire week, and eating a single bowl of Cap'n Crunch will shred the roof of your mouth into bloody ribbons. So how strong are we, really?

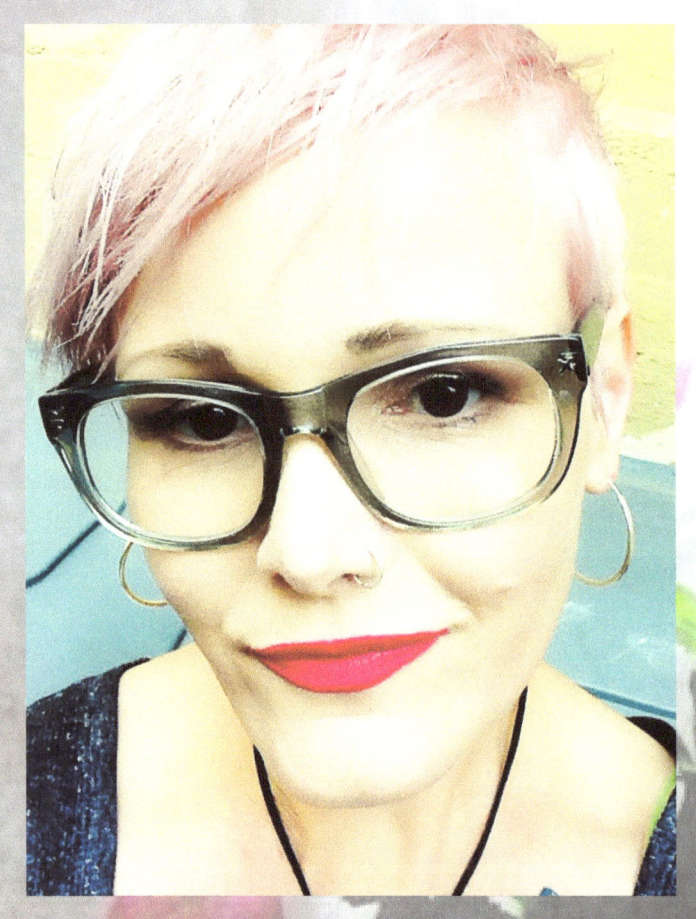

Author Bio

Corbyn has been a writer since she could string four words together. Sometimes she even gets paid to do it. In her past, she has worked as a manager of a money-laundering deli for the Israeli mob, an assistant for a washed-up cigar-smoking Broadway producer, and also enjoyed a brief stint as an amateur chicken farmer. She is wondering if 43 is too old to begin a career in burlesque. Her work has appeared in The Huffington Post, The New York Times, and More Magazine.

Artist Bio

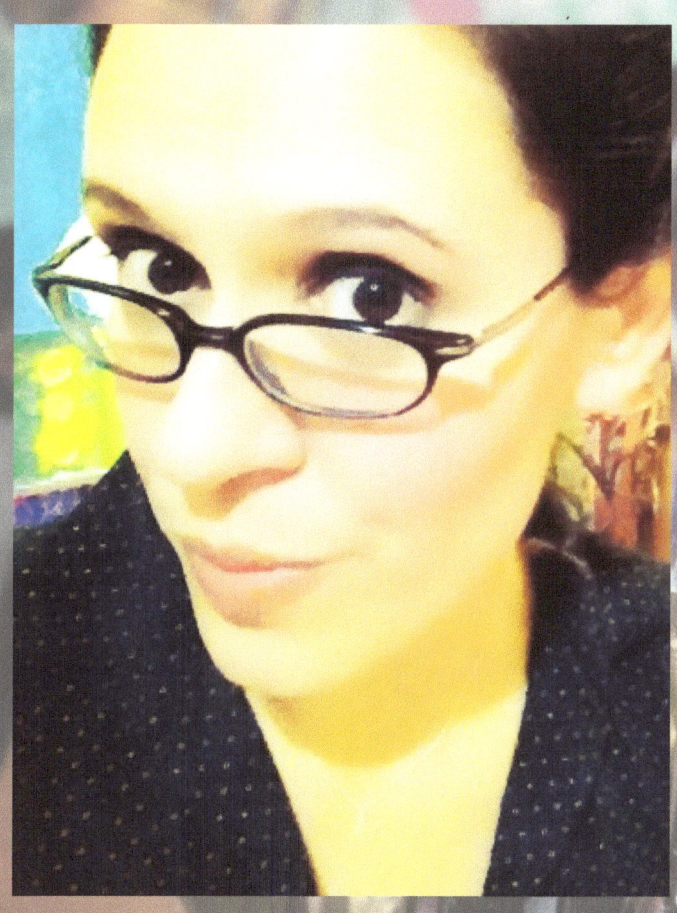

valeri may have been an artist before she started coloring outside the lines but it took her more than 30 years to actually call herself one. she received two degrees that have nothing to do with art but, along the way, took as many art history and art studio courses as she could. some of her favorite hobbies include spending a great deal of time contemplating both the transient and eternal nature of all things, seeing the magnificent in the mundane, and exploring the themes of life, death, and re-birth as they relate to the human experience. her artwork hints at such inquiry but is also full of innocence and wonder, with a curiously melancholic touch of darkness infused into otherwise playful pieces. she says it has something to do with balance. her work has appeared in galleries and boutiques in the US, as well as private collections throughout the US, UK, and Canada. valeri resides where the wild things are with her husband, three boys, and rambunctious pup.

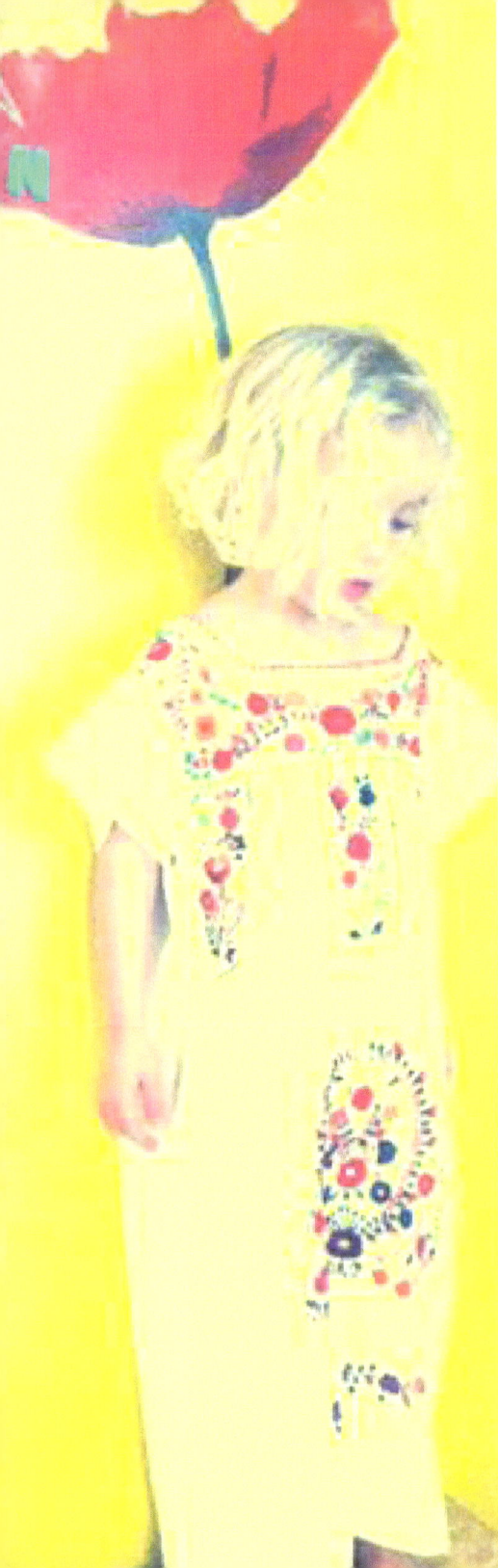

Acknowledgments

My name is Corbyn and I'm a writer. That's something I was almost ashamed to say aloud when I was younger, even though from as far back as I can remember, I knew it was what I was made to do. It was the only baked-in skill I really had (though I later learned how to parallel park like a MUTHA,) and I carried it around in my pocket like a smooth rock I could use to comfort myself during a rough childhood where school was a tough place to be, and home even tougher.

But I sought my solace in libraries, and it was there where I learned the magic writers can bring to an empty space, a hurting space, or to a growing brain that needs to know there's a world far beyond one that is small and painful. Books are magic. Writing is a gift of wizardry.

I wrote a memoir about my family's slide from financial comfort to poverty: the nightmare scenario of many parents. I scrapped most of it, and what you see here is what floated to the top.

I acknowledge the inspiration of music, my first and greatest love, from the bands my dad introduced me to in the seventies (that still occupies most of the space on my mental radio station), and then on into indie, rap, etc. Music leads me and I follow. My writing is inspired by the poetic lyrics of Joni Mitchell, of Stevie Nicks and Heart, the angry beat jazz of Gil Scott-Heron, the college influences of Pavement, the Velvet Underground, Big Star, hip hop greats like A Tribe Called Quest and Tupac Shakur, and on and on.

People who have supported my writing from the start: teacher Robert Feinstein, friends Evan Kalimtgis, Melissa Pecullan, and countless readers of my Facebook musings, blog posts, and articles. I was blessed with the mentor of any writer's DREAMS: Ms. Lisa Belkin. I thank old friend Jeremy Smith who first printed my work for pay, I bow humbly to artistic collaborator Valeri Blossom, my baby brother Randall Rothgeb who is the type who'll help me bury the body and ask questions later, my gentle husband and the rest of our little family who tolerate my job and its vicissitudes, my mate Alec who came through to heroically lay out this book in the eleventh hour... and so many more.

And all the writers, and all the books, and all the libraries I've loved. You didn't just build me, you saved me.

-Corbyn Hanson Hightower

first and foremost, i want to thank my husband. he not only didn't laugh at me or tell me that my dream was impossible but he made space for that dream by having an addition built on our first little house. for years i let kids' toys dominate that space, but little by little, i took action + painted in that space as well. sometimes with a baby on my back.

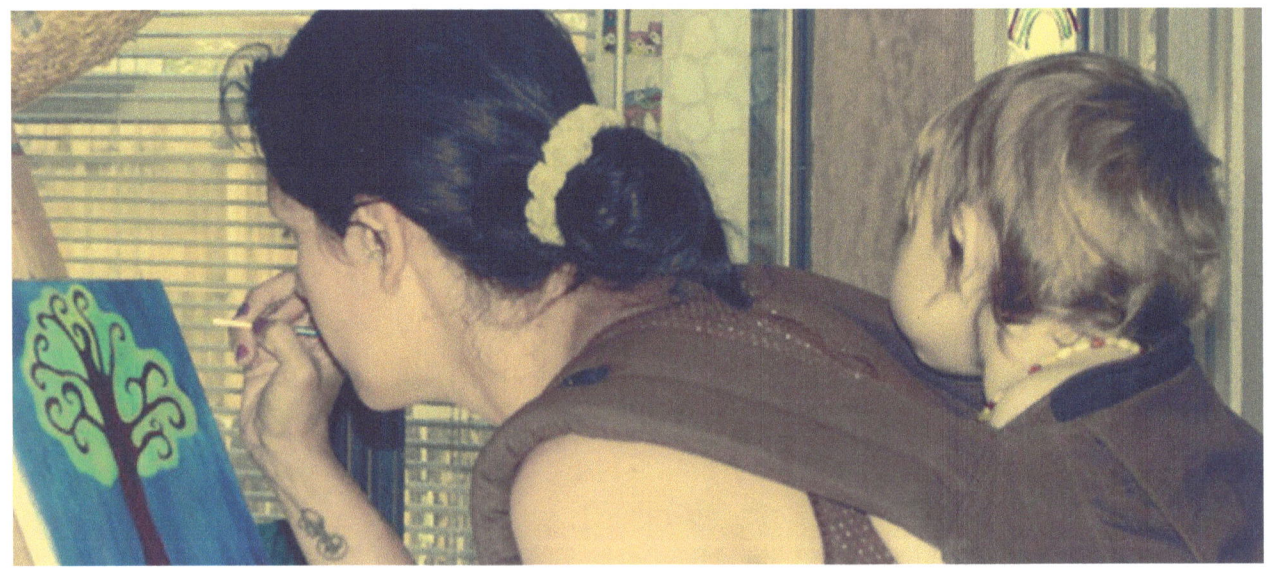

my eternal gratitude also goes out to my sisters, not related through blood but by blood: emily (often referred to as the wife for seeing me and allowing herself to be seen in the best and the worst of times) for being my constant creative consultant, katykins for dreaming and scheming with me and listening to me prattle on for the last twelve years, and bethyboo for believing in me, supporting me, and reminding me to laugh, be silly, and to breathe.

of course, my immense gratitude extends to corbyn for loving me and my work as much as I love her and hers, for bearing with me, and for editing my self-portraits in her most magical way and to alec, for being the stem of our fragile flower and helping us get our first book off the ground.

this section would not be complete without giving a shout out to some of my favorite people for paving the way with their inspiration and influence. it all started in a primary school library, the only place besides the nurse's office that i could seek comfort, thanks to the words of shel silverstein, the familiar faces of dr. seuss, and the wonderment of maurice sendak's work.

finally, i want to thank the stars for my amazingly brilliant boys who have taught (and continue to teach) me more than i could probably ever teach them, modest mouse for being my creative, philosophical soundtrack for the last decade, and for everyone i've crossed paths with thus far. it's not been easy but it has been worth it.

-valeri blossom

Take that silver lining and color in the whole damn cloud. Use that awesome crayon—the one that got flattened first in every box I ever owned.

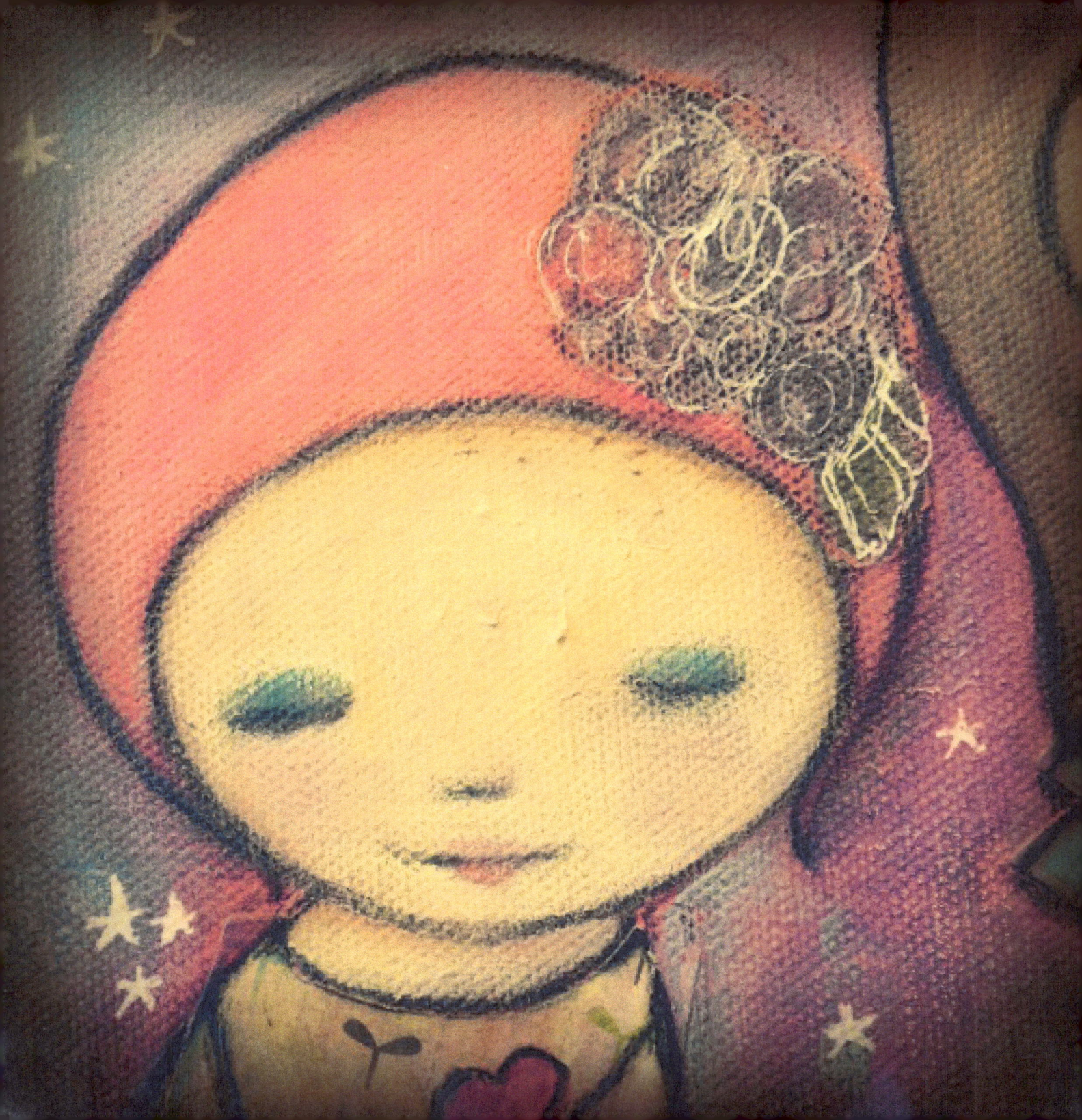

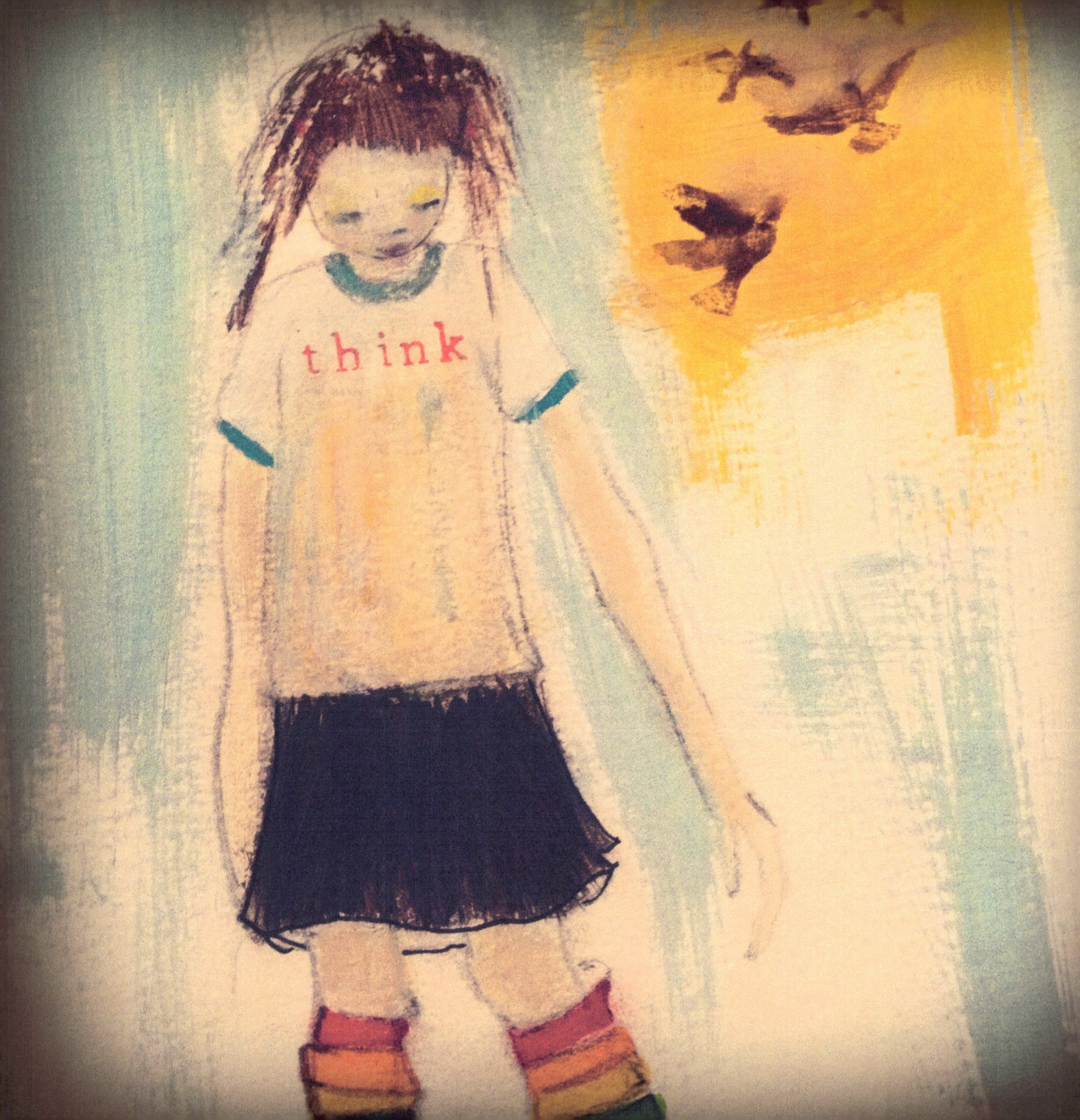

www.ingramcontent.com/pod-product-compliance
Lightning Source LLC
Chambersburg PA
CBHW050854180526
45159CB00007B/2672

* 9 7 8 0 6 1 5 9 5 6 8 3 1 *